Whether you are in a big or small c̳ gives invaluable insight into the opportunitites available for strengthening men. *How to Build a Life-Changing Men's Ministry* is a book in tune with the times and the heart of God.

JOSEPH M. STOWELL
President—Moody Bible Institute

As an athlete, I have always enjoyed learning from an experienced coach. From a guy who has been there. From someone able to share his knowledge with those around him. Steve Sonderman is that kind of leader. He doesn't talk from the press box. He's been actively involved in all facets of men's ministry—from missions to small group Bible studies, from large events to accountability groups. This book is a valuable play book for anyone involved in ministry to men.

JOHN ANDERSON
Former Professional Football Player

Steve Sonderman scores big with sound advice we can all put into practice in any men's ministry. Whether you're searching for a beginning or already have a group of guys meeting regularly, *How to Build a Life-Changing Men's Ministry* will have your team in the end zone and putting points on the board for eternity.

KEN RUETTGERS
Offensive Lineman—Green Bay Packers

HOW TO BUILD
A LIFE·CHANGING
MEN'S MINISTRY

Bringing the Fire
Home to Your Church

STEVE SONDERMAN

BETHANY HOUSE PUBLISHERS
MINNEAPOLIS, MINNESOTA 55438

Published by Bethany House Publishers
11400 Hampshire Avenue South
Bloomington, Minnesota 55438

Bethany House Publishers is a division of
Baker Publishing Group, Grand Rapids, Michigan.

Printed in the United States of America

ISBN-13: 978-1-55661-811-6
ISBN-10: 1-55661-811-5

Library of Congress Cataloging-in-Publication Data

Sonderman, Steve.
  How to build a life-changing men's ministry / Steve Sonderman.
      p. cm.

    1. Church work with men—United States.   2. Men—Religious
life—United States.   3. Men (Christian theology) I. Title.
BV4440.S66   1996
259'.081—dc20   96-10059
ISBN 1-55661-811-5   CIP

To Colleen

You are a gift from God.
I love you.

STEVE SONDERMAN is Associate Pastor for Men's Ministry at Elmbrook Church in Brookfield, Wisconsin. He consults widely with churches from a range of denominations in developing local men's ministries. Sonderman is a graduate of the University of Wisconsin—Milwaukee (B.S.) and Bethel Seminary (M.Div.). He makes his home in Wisconsin with his wife, Colleen, and four children.

Steve Sonderman is available to speak at retreats, rallies or other special events and to consult with your church or denomination about men's ministry. You can contact him at:

Steve Sonderman
Elmbrook Church
777 South Barker Road
Brookfield, WI 53045
(414) 786–7051

Contents

Riding the Crest of the Wave

I can still smell the summer of 1976.

As far as I was concerned, summer began in the middle of May and ended the first week of August—spanning the twelve weeks when our high school baseball team roared into the Wisconsin State Baseball Championship. A lot of the guys on the team had known each other since fourth grade, when we had started playing with or against one another in an assortment of city and county baseball leagues. With a potent mix of seniors, juniors and two sophomores, we started fast.

Then came a midseason slump. With ten games to go we were barely above the .500 mark. I blew out my right arm. Not that I had a strong arm in the first place—but an outfielder has to be able to throw. I was moved to DH. After a 12–0 shell-shocking at the hands of Homestead High School, we had a team meeting on the way home. It was an intense moment on the bus when we vowed to do whatever it took to turn the team around.

What a ride! We won our last ten games, including the state championship game against our archrival, Nicolet High School. Every game of the streak was better than the one before. We rode the crest of the wave. Great fielding. Deadly pitching. Incredible hitting. In the three-state tournament games we outscored our opponents 35–1. (The lone run was unearned.) I can still remember running onto the field and jumping into the air as the final out was made, hugging my teammates and crying like a baby and hoisting the Championship Trophy high into the sky. For years we had practiced and played in backyards and rocky fields through all types of weather to prepare for this day. We had come from many backgrounds, but what was important was that we had done it together. We were a team.

I won't forget the exhilaration and excitement of winning and being a part of something that felt enormously bigger than anything I had ever experienced.

I won't forget. But I've more than matched it.

In '76 we rode the crest of the wave to a state baseball championship. For the past five years I have been riding the crest of the wave with another team. Not a sports team. A ministry team—a *men's* ministry team. As I work shoulder to shoulder with other men on my leadership team, the exhilaration and excitement mimics the summer of '76. Tears flow when a man crosses over from trusting in his own goodness to make him acceptable to God to trusting Jesus as his Savior and Lord. My heart jumps up and down when I see men striving to be godly men in their homes, at work and in their communities. I get ecstatic when men start to use their spiritual gifts to ignite the local church. When men start to really get it. When they start to get excited about the things that excite Jesus.

We're seeing men's ministry happen today in many ways.

- Nine men sit around a table. They have one thing in common—unemployment. With the heart of a shepherd Doug listens as each man shares how he is dealing with the loss of his job and how the process of finding a new job is succeeding or failing. As Doug listens he provides words of comfort, encouragement and guidance. He feels their frustration, anger and sadness. He walks with them through this dark and difficult season of their lives. In the end he prays for them and promises to call during the week to see how they are doing. *This is men's ministry.*

- Four businessmen sit in an apartment in Suceava, Romania, talking with a team of leaders from a new and growing church. They discuss how these young believers, half of whom are unemployed, can start up a small business to employ ten people, support a pastor and bank money for a church in the future. The talk is about Christian business ethics, business plans, mission statements. The group brainstorms. The businessmen give the young believers an unusual freedom to think on their own. The room is electric as ideas start to flow and relationships develop. *This is men's ministry.*

- Twelve men gather in the conference room of a local construction company at 6:00 A.M. for their weekly "Top Gun" meeting. When they break into groups of four to share and pray for one another, Jim tells how he is thinking of leaving his wife. He says, "It's gone—the romance, the communication, the fun, the relationship. I just cannot go on any longer." For the next hour the other men listen, encourage and pray for Jim. He leaves at 7:45 A.M. with a renewed commitment to make his marriage work—to do whatever he can to get his marriage back. And in time he does. *This is men's ministry.*

- It is Wednesday noon and Dave isn't doing lunch with one more client or dashing home to have lunch with his wife. Dave instead closes his office door and spends his lunch hour fasting and praying for the men of his church and city. He petitions God that men would come to know Jesus. That men's hearts would love Jesus again. That the Christians in his city would be a part of the solution to the community's rampant racism. He prays for his pastor as he prepares for his weekly sermon. David is part of a larger group

of men who have committed to pray and fast every
Wednesday noon throughout the year. *This is men's ministry.*

- After a chicken barbecue a couple of hundred men settle
into their seats to listen to lively music by a local bluegrass
band. This is followed by a time of worship, a short drama,
a testimony and the introduction of the evening speaker.
The speaker happens to be Patrick Morley, businessman
and author of *The Man in the Mirror.* Everything has been
orchestrated to lead up to this time when Pat shares his
testimony and clearly explains what it means to be a Christian man in our society today. In the end he invites men to
respond to Jesus for the first time. Those who have brought
co-workers and friends nervously pray that their guest
would take the step. Many that night accept the free gift of
grace and commit all that they are to all that He is. *This is
men's ministry.*

- Mark, a pediatric doctor, sutures a five-inch gash on a
young boy's leg. What makes this a little different for Mark
and the other thirteen members of the team is that they are
working in a place called Kabankalan in the Philippines.
The boy had been cutting sugar cane with an eighteen-inch
machete and accidentally slashed his leg wide open. Mark
fixes him up. Working in primitive conditions, Mark sees
more than 200 children in just one week. Most come from
mountainous regions and have never been to a doctor.
Mark rides an emotional roller coaster. Many of the young
children he diagnoses and treats he sends on their way.
Others are beyond help. Thousands of miles from home
and the niceties of his local practice, Mark is doing what
he does best: taking care of kids. *This is men's ministry.*

- A local Greek restaurant is the meeting place for John's appointment. Just that morning John called a friend and
asked him to lunch. John asks how his friend is doing. For
the next hour John listens as Nate tells him how tough
work is. Nate feels overwhelmed. He isn't sure he's in the

right job. Should he stay? Should he move on? Finally he has found someone who cares for him as a man and not just a piece of property. He's able to share his heart, his fears, his true feelings. At the end of the hour John and Nate pray for each other and go back into the marketplace refreshed, refocused and recharged. *This is men's ministry.*

Those are the things this book is all about. It is about men. Ministering to men. Building a *team* of men able to do the ministry. It is a tool to help lay leaders within a local church start and run an effective men's ministry.

If ever there was a time in history when local churches needed to build men individually and corporately it is now. As we survey our country's spiritual and societal landscape, it becomes apparent not only that men need ministries made for them but that men are looking for them as well. Jesus once talked to His disciples about finishing the work that the Father had given Him to do. He then challenged the disciples to look at the fields—to notice that they were ripe, ready to be harvested (John 4:34–38).

Christ's challenge to us is to turn our eyes to the fields and see the opportunities before us. We can be tempted to anger that our world seems to be going from bad to worse. Yet what we see as problems in our society, we must grasp as opportunities for ministry.

Wherever I look I see men who desperately need a ministry uniquely designed to reach them *as men*, working at the issues they deal with. For a moment let's look at the fields. Let's see why men are ripe for harvest:

The American Male Is Friendless

Competition, comparison, isolation, individualism and self-sufficiency—those words describe today's American men. That isn't good news for men trying to make friends! Those are wedge-driving words. Splintering words. Those are labels most of us have worn since the day we were born—and as a result the average male over thirty can't name one close friend he could call at any time of the day or night to share his hurt and pain.

A recent survey asked men who their best friends were. More than 75 percent said it was a guy from high school, a guy from an old sports team, and so on. What was interesting is that most of the men hadn't spoken to that man or seen that man for several years. Some friendship.

The Lone Ranger of the '60s and '70s is looking for companionship in the '90s. He is looking for one or two good buddies to hang out with. Friends he can share heart to heart with. Friends who will walk with him at the birth of his first child, who will be there when he loses his job, who will provide wise counsel when his teenager rebels and mourn with him when his parents or spouse dies. In his wonderful book *Disciplines of a Godly Man*, Kent Hughes says this about male friendship: "Men, if you are married, your wife must be your most intimate friend, but to say 'my wife is my best friend' can be a cop-out. You also need Christian male friends who have a same sex understanding of the serpentine passages of your heart who will not only offer counsel and pray for you, but will also hold you accountable to your commitments and responsibilities when necessary."[1]

Men, look at the fields, they are ripe for harvest! What an opportunity for you to develop a ministry that helps men belong and to develop friendships. Where they can get together and get to know each another.

The American Male Is Emotionally Isolated

Herb Stanelle, counselor for men, says, "Emotional isolation can be viewed as the systematic separation of a person from his feelings. It is the process whereby a man changes from an eight-pound 'cherub' who coos, laughs, screams, cries and drools into a 200-pound 'humanoid' for whom all of life is work and all problems have intellectual, rational solutions."[2] The emotionally isolated male doesn't see himself as a creation wonderfully made by God but the sum of what he does at home, work and church.

That's the male self in a nutshell.

When men are asked what they are feeling, most give only a blank stare in return. Or they say they're "doing good" or "doing bad" (neither of which is a feeling). The price men are paying for ignoring their emotions is huge. It affects us physically. We suffer migraines, heart problems and ulcers—to pick just a few common problems. It affects us relationally. We are unable to nurture our wives and to relate to them on an emotional basis, perhaps their most vital need. Gary Oliver notes in *Real Men Have Feelings Too*: "When emotional pain strikes, we often lack the ability to understand and deal with it. When the pain becomes too uncomfortable, the only other option is to attempt to anesthetize it. For instance, you can replace feelings with busyness. The busyness becomes workaholism. They become insensitive and blind to their spouse's messages of discouragement, dissatisfaction and resentment."[3] From childhood the message we have heard is *men do not show emotions*. Big boys don't cry. To be a man is to conceal emotion.

The men I run with are saying those messages are wrong. The American male, while generally emotionally isolated, is looking to fully understand how God wired him. He is seeking to uncover the emotions stashed away inside himself and to find ways to express those gut-level feelings in a positive and healthy manner.

Leaders of men, look at the fields. They are ripe. What an incredible challenge to develop a ministry where men can be real and transparent—to develop small group ministries where men can share the three *F's*—feelings, failures and fears!

The American Male Is Confused Over Masculinity

What does it mean to be a man? It isn't hard to understand why we're confused. Every ten years our role model has changed. In the '60s it was James Bond, the womanizer. In the '70s it was Alan Alda and Phil Donahue, the sensitive and caring man. In the '80s it was Michael Douglas, the work-obsessed marketplace man, and now in the '90s it is Kevin Costner, aggressive yet ethical, traditional yet adventurous, intimate but independent, a family man developing a rich inner life. Worse yet, we haven't just watched these defective role models on TV and the big screen—we lived with them at home. Many of us grew up with fathers who were emotionally cold, uncommunicative or absent.

Chuck Swindoll, in *Growing Wise in Family Life*, says this: "I'm concerned about a vanishing masculinity that once was in abundance. I mean honest-to-goodness men who are distinctly that—discerning, decisive, strong-hearted men who know where they are going and are confident enough in themselves and their God to get there. Over the last three decades there has been an assault on masculinity."[4]

It's no wonder that men have an identity crisis. But men are searching for answers. They want to know what it means to be a man. They are buying books like *Fire in the Belly* by Sam Keen and *Iron John* by Robert Bly. They are attending Warrior Weekends by the hundreds. More men are seeking out therapists than ever before.

Men, lift your eyes to see the harvest. Men are ripe. What an opportunity to present the biblical base of man! We can present Jesus as the ultimate man, the man who knew who He was, where He came from and where He was going. What an opportunity to help searching men discover their identity in Christ Jesus!

The American Male Is Success Driven

Climbing the ladder. Promotions. A bigger home. Nicer car. That prime corner office with floor-to-ceiling windows. Winning the big one.

The competitive nature within each of us just wants more. We have become convinced that *what we do* is *who we are*.

How much we have and how fast we get it determine our status in society. Wherever we look we see men moving faster and faster, seeking to do more and more in order to leap higher and higher. We are obsessed with success. Success means status and position—and that's what it's all about.

Once again, the price men are paying for this obsession to succeed is enormous. With the pressure to succeed, our commitment to choose right over wrong has vanished. The success obsession also exacts a price from families. When a man pours all of his attention and energy into work he has nothing left for home. When he arrives home after 10–12 hours at the office he has come home physically—but not mentally or emotionally. His relationship with his wife suffers. His relationships with his children withers. Most marriages end in divorce not because of a mistress *at* work but a mistress *called* work.

Are the fields ever ripe for harvest! Men everywhere are realizing that there has to be a better way. As the old adage goes—they have been climbing the ladder for a good part of their life and when they reached the top they realized the ladder was leaning against the wrong wall. When I surveyed 500 men about the biggest issue they were facing in life, this was the most frequent cry by far: *How do I balance home and work?* What an opportunity to build a ministry where men can study biblical principles of work, home and recreation—and to grow a group of men who will hold one another accountable for how they spend their time, energy and money!

The American Male Today Is Spiritually Searching

There is no way to ignore the fact that in the summer of 1995 more than 700,000 men attended Promise Keepers Conferences around the country, with even more expected in the future. And at each of the thirteen conferences hundreds of men came forward after the first talk either to make an initial commitment to Christ or to make a recommitment.

The obvious question men ask themselves after a great

weekend of teaching, worship and fellowship is this: *What's next? How do I continue this and grow in it?* The only way to bring the fire home is to grow a strong, healthy men's ministry in every local church. Our isolated retreats or conferences or mission projects pose an obvious danger. Men can have a great experience and then come home and slide into old routines— or even worse, get inoculated with just enough Christianity to give them a false sense of security.

The number of books, magazines and tapes on spiritual growth and men's issues being bought today is another sign of male spiritual hunger. In the past it has been women who have kept most Christian bookstores in business. Today more men are buying Christian materials than ever before. When I visit our bookstore it seems there is a new men's book out just about every week. The spiritual hunger of men is changing the Christian book industry.

The ongoing debate over family values is another sign that men are looking for something different from what society has portrayed as normal. Presidential hopefuls speak of values. William Bennett's books explain them. The media is confused by them. But one thing is true. Most Americans desire them in their life and family. They are searching for what is right.

Let me say it just one more time: Leaders of men, lift up your eyes, for the fields are ripe for harvest! Men are ready to be built together in a ministry designed to connect Christ with their real daily needs. Men today are ready to get into small groups where they can help each other grow into Christ's like- ness. Where they can talk about ways to raise godly children in a godless society. Where they can meet on a regular basis to worship with other men through song and prayer. Men today are searching. We have an incredible opportunity before us.

Building a Life-Changing Men's Ministry

For the past twelve years I have served as an associate pas- tor at Elmbrook Church in Brookfield, Wisconsin. For the past five years I have been responsible for our Men's Ministry. The ministry has grown from 50 to 500 men involved weekly, with one local meeting attracting 4,500 men. The leadership team has grown from 8 to 96. I also consult with churches of all sizes and denominations on how to start and run effective men's ministries.

Men's ministry is finally coming home to the church. Nothing is greater in life than working with men in this environment. God does use other means of ministering to men. But His primary means of reconciling the world to himself—men included—is the church. It is my prayer and dream that as you move through this book you will catch the vision and passion of what can happen when men come together to serve Jesus together.

This book will help you build a men's ministry within your church whether you are a lone individual or part of a small group of men; whether starting from scratch or adding to what you already have going. What I write applies to churches of 100 people, 1,000 people, even 10,000 people. The principles are the same, though the applications may be different. I have given points to ponder and exercises throughout that will help you to walk through the practical steps that make growing a men's ministry achievable.

I would suggest you work through the material together with other like-minded men, slowly enough to complete the exercises that apply to you and your situation. I have no intention of laying out a model and barking, "Copy it!" Rather I will give you straightforward principles, ideas and guidelines you can use to develop a ministry for your own setting.

Having done a stint as a high school football coach I still find myself thinking and talking like a coach. Besides that, there are almost endless similarities between building a team and building a ministry. For those reasons I have decided to attack this book like I would a football season. In the first chapters we will prep for the season, then move into developing a coaching staff, scouting out the players, setting a game plan, kicking off and playing the game—everything you need to know to get from here to the end zone.

No matter where you are right now in developing your ministry you need to know where you're going. In the next chapter we will look at what the biblical man looks like. So let's get started.

Notes

1. Kent Hughes, *Disciplines of a Godly Man* (Wheaton, Ill.: Crossway Books, 1991), p. 61.
2. Herb Stanelle, "The Emotionally Isolated Christian Male," article from *Social Work and Christianity*, Vol. 18, No. 2 (Fall 1991), p. 1.
3. Gary Oliver, *Real Men Have Feelings Too: Regaining a Male Passion for Life* (Chicago: Moody Press, 1993), p. 63.
4. Chuck Swindoll, *Growing Wise in Family Life* (Portland, Ore.: Multnomah Press, 1988).

What Are We Aiming At?

Youth Soccer. Everywhere I look in our community on Saturday mornings there are kids running around playing soccer—and adults screaming on the sidelines as if they were at the Super Bowl. In our community alone there are 1,800 kids playing this fall.

Having grown up on football, basketball and baseball—and then coaching high school football for five years—I swore I would have nothing to do with soccer. No playing. No watching. No letting my kids play it. And the ultimate—I would never, ever coach it!

For the past two years I have been coaching soccer.

It went like this. My two daughters came home from school with a registration form for the local youth soccer league. That was bad enough. Then came the tactic all kids are taught in "kid school"—"Dad, they said they're short of coaches, and if you don't coach the team may not be able to play." *Great. Solved that problem. I guess my kids won't be playing soccer.*

But then my soft side took over my brain. I said, "Sure, I would love to help."

I went to the library and took out all the books and videos I could find on soccer. Of course I had a twofold agenda. First,

I could learn all about this game I knew nothing about. Second, if I had all the books none of the other rookie coaches could study up. (Yes, I am very competitive.)

At the first practice I sat down with the twelve kids and said, "Okay, kids. You need to know that I have never played, watched or coached this game, but there are two things I know. First, this is a ball. The second thing I know is that over there is a goal." I pointed to the goal behind me. "The one thing we want to do this year is to get this ball in that net. That's the goal. I don't care where you run around. I don't care how you kick it, or where you kick it—just get it into that goal. I don't know how we're going to do it. But, girls, that's what we're going to try to do."

It's not a whole lot different in ministry. We need to know where we're going. What's our goal? What kind of men do we want to grow? Ministry needs to be principle-centered and purpose-driven. We can run a lot of programs, we can stage a lot of events, we can burn through as many Bible studies as we want—but unless we know where we're going, we will never get there.

As we saw in the first chapter, we have incredible opportunities right now to develop men's ministries in the local church. Yet the men we want to grow strong in God have been warped and misshapen by their world. They have been influenced by their society. Most have made countless poor decisions. And they are greatly confused about what it means to be a man—much less a biblical man. One of the first projects for your leadership team is to talk and pray through how God sees men and how that affects your goals in ministry.

So who is this biblical man? What should the end product of our ministry be? If you and I could take a piece of paper and sketch the ideal man, what would he really look like?

The guy we are aiming at has four characteristics: integrity, intimacy, identity and influence. As we understand these four marks of a mature godly man, we begin to see what type of ministry it takes to build that man.

Men of Integrity

Len Climber became president of Holiday Inn International in 1973. As corporate president he wanted one thing: for people who heard or saw the name "Holiday Inn" to instantly think "Good, wholesome, family fun." Climber did everything in his power not only to sell a company image but to shape a company culture worthy of that image. Through the '70s he made Holiday Inn the fastest growing, largest hotel chain in the country.

In 1977 Climber resigned. Why? His board decided to connect a Holiday Inn to an Atlantic City casino. They violated his code for the company. They overran his conscience.

Climber's resignation cost him millions. An interviewer asked him why he left Holiday Inn. "It was very, very easy," he replied. "It had to do with my integrity."[1]

Biblical men are men of *integrity*. "Integrity" comes from the Hebrew word for "whole," "sound," "unimpaired." It means to possess a genuine heart. It evidences itself in ethical soundness, moral excellence, absence of hypocrisy and a willingness to keep promises. No hidden messages. No hidden agendas. A man of integrity is true to his word. Like Len Climber, they say, "This is what I stand for. This is what I believe. This is right. If you want to do something else, fine. But I will have nothing to do with it."

Little in society is under more fire than the character quality of integrity. Its absence is felt in government, the military, sports, business and yes, even the church. The integrity crisis is a national emergency. Kenneth Blanchard, author of *The One-Minute Manager* and *The Power of Ethical Management*, observes: "All across our country, there is evidence of a deterioration of ethics. Nowhere is this decline greater than in the world of business. . . . Individuals seemingly have come to check their values at the door when they enter the office. The attitude in many businesses appears to be profit at any cost, especially if a company's gains come at the expense of a competitor—and sometimes, even if it is at the expense of its customers."[2]

Integrity will show itself in the men of our ministry in three ways.

Integrity shows in convictions. Through study, encouragement and accountability we want to help men to become men of conviction—men who know what they believe in and act on it. What went through your mind when you saw on television or in news magazines the nineteen-year-old student who held up his hands to stop a tank in China's Tienanmen Square? Conviction. That young guy was ready to pay the ultimate price because he knew the rightness of what he believed in. Shortly after Tienanmen Square you saw high school- and college-age students with pickaxes knocking down the Berlin Wall—with armed soldiers pointing guns at their heads. That's conviction. That's what I want. I want to be a man of conviction. And that's what we want to develop.

Integrity shows in congruence. We want to develop men whose walk matches their talk. Eighty-one percent of what we communicate to our kids and to our wives is conveyed by what we do. We cannot settle for men who look good at church but who everywhere else lie, cheat and sleep around. We need to help men develop consistency between what they profess on Sunday and how they act at work, home and in their neighborhoods Monday through Saturday.

Integrity shows in character. Many men can masquerade on Sundays. They can disguise their sins, failings and weaknesses and look good from the outside. Some men can manage that deception in front of their families and co-workers. But who are our men when no one is looking? Do they cheat on their taxes? Do they lead double lives? Do they stumble with pornography—or lust or greed or covetousness or other sins of the hidden heart? Our ministry needs to build men who are strong because they have come to grips with their brokenness and been healed.

Points to Ponder:
1. Where is a lack of integrity most clearly seen in our community?
2. What integrity issues do the men of our church deal with?
3. How is integrity developed? What must we include in our ministry to help our guys become men of integrity?
4. How is my integrity as a leader? What steps can I take to grow in that area?

Men of Intimacy

The second mark of the biblical man is *intimacy*. "Intimacy" comes from the Latin word *intus*, "within." It's a sharing of life with another. It's allowing others into our heart— the inner chamber. It's journeying into their heart. And it means we become one.

We want to help men develop intimacy in three areas of life.

The biblical man experiences intimacy with God. I'll be blunt. We all have a lot of guys in our churches who come on Sunday mornings because their wives drag them there. Their whole idea of Christianity is playing church. So what's the problem? They're settling for secondhand religion. They're just going through the motions—stand up, sit down, throw a buck in the plate. They're missing out on an authentic, growing, vital, living relationship with Jesus Christ.

Men move beyond the motions when they realize God made them to know Him—even deeper than that, to commune with Him. To enjoy Him. To experience Him. Made *by* God *for* God. They can know what it means to wake up in the morning, jump out of bed and onto their knees and say "God, thank you so much for the life you've given me." They can enjoy God's presence moment by moment, day by day by day. Not just punch the clock for an hour on Sunday morning. We want to work toward that end.

The biblical man experiences intimacy with his wife. Men need help to see their marriage as more than "the marriage

thing," something to scratch off the to-do list of life. Men
spend a lot of time and energy and money courting and dating.
We write letters. We phone. We buy flowers. We do anything
to catch the woman we want. Then we get married, have our
awards banquet, go on the honeymoon . . . and it's over. What's
next? What's the next project, the next deal, the next hill to
climb? We drop our marriages and leave our wives behind.
Most of us stay married, but as far as our time and energy and
money are concerned, the marriage thing is done. And our
wives feel it.

A biblical man realizes intimacy with his wife is both deep
and wide. It's deep. It's a sharing of hearts. It's a journey into
the deepest cavern of who man and woman are, an exploration
of what it means to become soul mates. But his intimacy with
his wife is also wide. It encompasses their entire relationship.
It's emotional—laughing and crying together. It's social—dating, going out together, having people over. It's intellectual—
reading, sharing ideas, discussing politics, talking about life
and life issues. It's physical—holding hands, touching bodies.
It's spiritual—praying together, worshiping together. Intimacy
between a husband and wife involves all that they are—sharing dreams, hopes, fears, failures. And slowly—through small
groups, through one-on-one counsel—we want to rock a man's
view of marriage, to help him move beyond "the marriage
thing" to experience real intimacy. Total-*person* contact with
his wife.

For the first five years of my marriage we had a rule in our
house: "Don't rock the boat." I was busy. I had been called to
our church to start a college-age ministry. Everything I did re-
volved around the start-up, working day and night to guar-
antee a good ministry. So when I went home my rule was "Colleen, don't talk to me about your problems or the kids'
problems or home problems." And my wife's rule was "Steve,
don't talk about work. I don't want to hear more of your ideas,
more of your plans, more of your strategies. You always have
a new vision and I don't want to hear another one."

That was our rule for five years. One day I came home and she met me at the door—that was new. She said, "I have great news." And I said, "So, it was a great trade, huh? Who was it—the Packers, the Brewers or the Bucks?" It had to be sports-related. That was the only good news I was waiting for. She said, "No, it's none of those." Well, we already had two children, so I guessed. "Okay. Number three's on the way." She said, "No, it's not number three." I said, "No trades, no pregnancy, what's left?" She said, "I'm going to rock the boat." I said, "You're gonna what?" She said, "Sit down, honey." I sat down. She said, "Steve, I don't like your lifestyle. I don't like the way you work. I don't like your habits. And we're going to change all this." I said, "Oh, welcome home. It's really been a great five minutes."

We sat down that night and had a very long conversation. For the first time I shared with her my greatest fear—the fear I had kept stuffed inside me my whole life. I was afraid of failure. I had never told *anyone* that. And through a lot of crying and kicking and hugging that long evening we moved past the "Hi, how are ya? Everything's fine, honey" kind of relationship. We sank the don't-rock-the-boat rule. We shared our hearts. We shared life. We broke through to intimacy.

Real ministry takes place when you move men toward intimacy. When you can explain to them what's going on in their hearts so they can open up with their wives to share feelings, failures, what's really going on inside.

The biblical man experiences intimacy with other men. It's one thing to have intimacy with God. It's another thing to have intimacy with a wife. The biblical man needs one more thing. He learns to open up to other men, to have male friendships.

If you look at the Bible you'll see that the guys God used surrounded themselves with other men. *Moses.* Who did Moses have? Aaron. *Joshua?* Caleb. *David?* Jonathan. The story in 1 Samuel 18 describes a wonderful friendship in the making. God actually knit the souls of David and Jonathan. They became one in spirit. What about *Jesus*? He had the three—Peter, James, John—and the rest of the twelve. What about *Paul*? Barnabas, Timothy, Luke. Everywhere you look you see men surrounding themselves with other men.

We have built our ministry around Proverbs 27:17, "As iron sharpens iron, so one man sharpens another." What we're about is helping men to connect with other men. As I noted in the first chapter, most men don't have friends. We can put them in situations where they can at least begin to break down walls and get to know one another, draw on one another and depend on one another. Christianity isn't a solo sport. In the same way it would be suicide to climb Mt. Everest by yourself, so it is spiritual suicide to try to make it on your own spiritually.

Until seven years ago I had never been in a small group. I was a pastor—and I never gave it much thought. But following that conversation with Colleen I realized I had some problems in my life and needed to be more intimate with her and with other people. I asked three guys to be in a small group with me. Seven years ago we covenanted to meet an hour a week to talk about what was going on in our lives and to ask ourselves the tough questions. It's been encouraging. When things got tough with our marriages or our kids or our ministries, we could call day or night. It's been challenging. They see my blind spots, sins I was pushing off. They could look me in the face and say, "Shape up!" When I was lying they knew it. And they weren't afraid to call me on it.

We need to develop situations where men can get into those types of relationships. It's the "So what?" factor. We can take 20 guys or 30 guys to a large men's conference like Promise Keepers and they get stoked. Then they come home and say, "So what? What's next? What do we do the 51 other weekends?" By placing men in small groups we can move them into intimate relationships that challenge them, help them grow and give them a sense of belonging.

We have a long way to go to build men of intimacy. As males we seem bred for independence. We isolate ourselves behind big, thick walls. I've tried to jackhammer through some of those walls with guys and it's hard. Walls don't break down quickly. But there's nothing more exciting than seeing those walls slowly come down.

Points to Ponder:

1. What do you see as obstacles to intimacy for the men you work with?

   Intimacy with God:

   Intimacy with their wife:

   Intimacy with other men:

2. What will you need to incorporate into your ministry to help men grow in these three areas?

3. How are you doing in these areas of your life? What steps must you take to relight the fire in your relationship with:

   Your God:

   Your Wife:

   Other Men:

Men of Identity

In an era when both John Wayne toughness and Alan Alda sensitivity seem limiting, the Bible offers us positive role models and principles that show us what true masculinity is all about. The biblical man is balanced. The biblical man is complete. The biblical man is certain of his *identity*.

You can see men struggle with their identity whenever they gather. Question number one—*What's your name?*—is

immediately, inevitably followed by question number two—
What do you do? As someone so nicely said, male identity in
our culture is usually based on one of the four *B's*—brains,
brawn, bucks or beauty.[3]

My wife has a simple equation she uses to describe me.
When I start sharing my struggles and what's going on, she'll
say, "Steve Sonderman equals numbers."

I know I'm like a lot of men. I'm results-oriented. I love my
work. If I don't watch it I start telling myself *I am what I do.*
Other guys measure their worth by sales, quotas and titles. I
track how many guys showed up for a meeting. Yet our significance isn't in what we do. In God's system, our identity
comes from Christ. There are four biblical principles we can
remind our men of right from the start:

We have been created by God for God. In Psalm 139:14 it
says "[we] are fearfully and wonderfully made." We can help
our men realize they are unique, specially designed by God.
There is no one in the world exactly like them. Their personality, temperament and physical body are unique. In God's
eyes they are important because He created them.

Christ loved us enough to die for us. John 3:16 tells us that
God sent His Son to die for us. If our men ever question
whether God loves them, we can point them to the Cross. It is
the greatest definition and most powerful reminder of God's
love we can imagine.

Christ lives in me. In Galatians 2:20 we are reminded that
if we have been crucified with Christ we no longer live but He
lives in us. He is in the process of making men into His image—and what He starts He will finish.

The masculinity of Jesus is our model. The masculinity of
Jesus Christ illustrates what *real* masculinity is. He was able
to cry and demonstrate incredible compassion. Yet He could
be tough as nails. He stood up for what He believed in. He
chased guys out of the synagogue. Tender, yes, but also tough.
He was a man's man. Brawny fisherguys followed him. When
people threw a party, who'd they invite? Jesus. He knew how

to have a good time and people liked to hang out with Him. Our men need to study the life of Jesus to meet the ultimate man.

We want to develop men who sense what biblically muscular, masculine Christianity is all about. Power under control. Strength clothed in tenderness. As you work with men on this level and use Scripture to reshape their attitudes, they will become all that God meant them to be. Their significance is not in what they do—though there's nothing wrong with that. Their value and identity are in Christ.

Points to Ponder:

1. What heroes or leaders do your men identify with? Who are they trying to become?

2. How as a leader are you reflecting the masculinity of Christ to your men?

Men of Influence

After having an incredible coaching career at the University of Oklahoma, Bud Wilkerson responded to a request to head up the President's Council on Physical Fitness. After a year on the job he called a press conference. One of the reporters asked him why football is good for this country. Everyone expected a ten-minute pep-talk on the greatness of football. Wilkerson's response was shocking. "Football," he said, "is terrible for this country." Why? "Football is 80,000 men desperately in need of exercise watching twenty-two men desperately in need of rest." That's just like the church. The church is hundreds and hundreds of men desperately in need of using their gifts watching a handful of guys, weary, exhausted from well-doing, who need a rest.

Take a man who won't settle for the status quo. A man who won't just go through the motions. A man who will leave his comfort zone and say, "I want to stand up. I want to be counted. I want to be a part of what God's doing." That's a man who will get out of the stands and onto the field. That's a man of *influence*.

Part of our goal is to train men to do ministry. And to train men to train *other* men to do ministry. We're not going to settle for just getting together to talk about our problems. We're not meant to be a holy huddle. I don't pay $30.00 to watch the Packers huddle. I go to see the Packers line up and butt heads. That's for us too! We have holy huddles. We get together for encouragement and growth and accountability. *Great*. But then we move out in society and do battle.

We're all concerned about changing our world and prevailing over the evils we see in society *right now*. We'll do that. But we also impact our world in unexpected ways—even after we die. We live on in two ways. We live on in eternity with Christ. We also live on in the lives we have influenced, the lives we have invested ourselves in. The first dozen verses of Psalm 78 describe how we as fathers are to teach our children, who in turn teach their children, who will in turn teach their children. What that passage describes is four generations of people being influenced by our actions today. Think about it! We can influence the children of the twenty-second century by investing our lives now. That's the potential of influence.

A man of influence sees the future. He sees the profit his investments will yield many years down the road. And so he pours his time and energy and money into people. Paul shows us how: "We loved you so much that we were delighted to share with you not only the gospel of God but our lives as well, because you had become so dear to us. Surely you remember, brothers, our toil and hardship; we worked night and day in order not to be a burden to anyone while we preached the gospel of God to you" (1 Thessalonians 2:8–9). We loved you so much, we shared not only the gospel, but our lives. That is ministry. Time and toil invested. The spectacular yield was yet to come.

Walt grew up on the streets of Philadelphia. When Walt became a Christian later in life he went to his church and volunteered to teach Sunday school. The church thought that was fine—but he had to find his own kids for the class. Walt went back to the streets. He found a bunch of kids playing marbles. He went to the first kid and asked how he'd like to come to his Sunday school class. The kid said sure. He wanted to know what they'd do. Walt told the boy that they would have an hour each Sunday to talk about the Bible and spend time together. Then Walt asked if the boy had any friends who would like to come. He pulled them all in. Thirteen guys.

For the next several years Walt stayed with those guys. Every Sunday he met with them, taught them, invested his life in them. He started having them over for dinner, going to their houses for dinner. Took them to the zoo, to a ball game. He started to invest all that he was with thirteen young boys.

A few years back, when Walt died, someone checked on what had happened to those thirteen guys. Today, eleven of the thirteen are in full-time Christian service. One of them is Howard Hendricks, Dean of Students at Dallas Theological Seminary—a man who knows what it is to influence men, a man who himself has discipled the next generation of men.[4]

The men we work with are going to live on in the people they invest their lives in. Dietrich Bonhoeffer says it well: "A righteous man is one who lives for the next generation." That's influence.

Points to Ponder:
1. Where are most of the men serving in your church?

2. Where is there need for men to serve?

3. How do you set up your ministry to equip, encourage and move men into service?

4. How did God work to get you involved in ministry?

See That? That's the Goal

So what's our goal? What are we shooting at? God wants us to build biblical men. That's the goal of our men's ministry. If we fail to produce men of integrity, intimacy, identity and influence we have failed to score. We've missed the net. The ball of men's ministry has rolled off the field, out into the street and been run over by a car. We have missed the chance to follow God and become strong in Him.

In the first chapter we saw where men are at. Now we've looked briefly at what God wants them to be. Here's the question now: How do we get men from where they are to where God wants them to be? The rest of this book is going to give you practical ways you and the men around you can build a life-changing men's ministry.

Notes

1. Ron Lee Davis, *Mentoring: The Strategy of the Master* (Nashville, Tenn.: Thomas Nelson, Inc., 1991), p. 102.
2. Kenneth Blanchard, quoted in Touche Ross, Touche Ross & Co., "Ethics in American Business: A Special Report," p. 37.
3. Patick Morley, *The Seasons of a Man's Life* (Nashville, Tenn.: Thomas Nelson, Inc., 1995), p. 269.
4. Howard Hendricks and William Hendricks, *As Iron Sharpens Iron* (Chicago: Moody Press, 1995), pp. 14–15.

Developing a Coaching Staff

Great teams almost always have great coaches. The championship teams I remember from growing up seemed to have one thing in common: a man at the head of the team superbly able to motivate and manage players. Players could come and go but the coaches remained the same. The Cowboys had Landry, the Dolphins had Shula, UCLA had Wooden, the Reds had Anderson, the Steelers had Knoll, Penn State had Paterno, the '49ers had Walsch, Carolina had Dean Smith and the Packers had Lombardi. They were all men who molded other men into winners, who shaped an environement where players worked and won together.

Growing up in Wisconsin, I heard Lombardi bedtime stories. "He treated us all the same," Ray Nitescke used to say of Lombardi. "Like dogs." Defensive tackle Henry Jordon says, "When Coach Lombardi tells me to sit, I don't even look for a chair." No player, no matter how gifted, could upstage Lombardi. "There are planes, trains and buses leaving Green Bay every day, and you may be on one of them," Lombardi used to say. It wasn't an empty threat. Jim Ringo, the Packers' phenomenal all-pro center, walked into Lombardi's office in 1963 and presented his agent. "Let me get this straight," said Lombardi. "You're his agent?" The hapless fellow nodded. The coach excused himself and walked into an adjoining room, returning a few minutes later. "I'm sorry," Lombardi said, turning to the agent. "You're talking to the wrong man. Jim Ringo is the property of the Philadelphia Eagles."

Lombardi was a coach who made things happen.

The Man Who Knows Where God Is Going

Whenever you start a sports team you start with the coach. He's the man who pulls together a staff, then the team. It's no different in ministry. In order to reach men you start with the leadership team—the coaches. More specifically, however, you need to start with one man who is going to head it up— the head coach.

This is a win-or-lose truth: Until you have a man willing to be the point person for your men's ministry you will have a difficult time making your ministry go. Until you have that person, in fact, you may want to hold off on starting your ministry. Richard Elsworth Day, in his book *Filled With the Spirit*, says this about the significance of key individuals in God's plans:

> It would be no surprise if a study of secret causes were undertaken to find that every golden era in human history proceeds from the devotion and righteous passion of some single individual. This does not set aside the sovereignty of God. It simply indicates the instrument through which He uniformly works. There are no bona fide mass movements. It only looks that way. At the center of the column there is always one man or woman who knows God and knows where He is going.[1]

Can you identify the head of your team? He may already be in place. The men of your church may be looking around at each other waiting for someone to take the lead. There's a good chance your leader is the guy holding this book—a man passionate about men's ministry. In this chapter we will look at the characteristics of the men you want leading your ministry and how to recruit them. The man who heads your ministry needs these general qualifications. They're what God expects of any maturing believer. But your head man also needs a clear vision of where God is going and the incredible harvest before us. He also needs some skill at leading, or at least a willingness to learn. Grab a pen and work through *Exercise 1—The Marks of a Leader.*

Exercise 1—The Marks of a Leader

1. Develop a list of ministries and movements of God that started with an individual. Think Bible, church history, revival and evangelistic movements, and significant happenings in your own church. List as many men as you can.

2. Pick five of the individuals you listed. What characteristic(s) made people follow him?

   Person: Key characteristic(s):
   (a)

   (b)

   (c)

   (d)

   (e)

3. What are the characteristics of men you want leading your men's ministry?

    (a)

    (b)

    (c)

    (d)

    (e)

4. Given your church's structure, who decides who will lead your men's ministry? Who's the pick?

Building the Team

It isn't enough to find one man who can see where God is going and motivate and manage a group of men to get there. You need men serving alongside that man. Building that *team* of leaders is the first big step in starting your men's ministry.

Ministry happens best in teams. A ministry team sets you up for quality ministry now and positions you for future growth. In his book *The Frog in the Kettle*, George Barna writes that "Leadership will be a key component if the church [or a men's ministry] is going to progress. Churches that grow in the

'90s will be those that have a strong but compassionate leadership team. They will be churches that are focused upon God's vision of ministry for them, and pursue it with passion and excitement."[2]

Aim to develop three to five men who will partner to form your key ministry team. There are five qualities to look for in the men you desire to lead your ministry.

Leaders With a Servant Spirit

In Mark 10:42–45, Jesus shares with His disciples the key element in spiritual leadership. He tells them the way *up* is *down*. He tells them the person who will lead is the one who will serve. Our society is obsessed with climbing the ladder, up-scaling, promotions and upward mobility. Jesus let it be known that those who will lead in the kingdom of God will be obsessed with descending the ladder, down-scaling, spiritual demotions and downward mobility. Those that lead will be a servant to all.

I have found it exceedingly easy to find men who want to be involved in ministry as long as they start at the top and don't have to do the ordinary, dirty jobs. They want to be up front teaching or around the table making decisions, not in the back making coffee or setting up chairs. Sometimes I get the impression some men feel they are above certain tasks. They import their marketplace position, power and philosophy and believe it will work in the church.

It doesn't and it shouldn't.

My ears perk up when a man says, "Steve, what needs to be done? Just name it!" Just the other day a man from our church who owns a huge construction company asked me if anything needed to be done. I told him we had a bulk mailing—2,600 pieces—to get out yesterday. "It's done," he said. He called a few guys, they met at church and went at it. I walked in late that night after another meeting and they were just finishing up. Here's a company president stuffing and licking envelopes. In his company he pays other people to do that. His servant spirit was contagious to the other guys.

That's the type of guy I want leading the ministry. The guy who understands to the core of his being that ministry is servanthood. I look for *FAT* guys. A man with a servant spirit is:

Faithful. Will he follow through on small jobs? Can he be trusted?

Available. Does he offer himself to be used, or are you always pulling him along?

Teachable. Is he willing to learn, or is he arrogant and unbending?

Getting a ministry going creates an enormous amount of work. Some tasks—making calls, compiling surveys, sending out mailings—are repetitious and menial. But they need to get done. One guy on your team who thinks he's above that kind of work breeds instant division.

Have your leadership team study together Henri Nouwen's book *In the Name of Jesus: Reflections on Christian Leadership.* In the book Nouwen says about servanthood, "Christian leadership in the future . . . is not leadership of power and control, but a leadership of powerlessness and humility in which the suffering servant of God, Jesus Christ, is made manifest . . . a leadership in which power is constantly abandoned in favor of love. . . . Powerlessness and humility in the spiritual life do not refer to people who have no spine and who let everyone else make decisions for them. They refer to people who are so deeply in love with Jesus that they are ready to follow Him wherever He guides them. . . ."[3]

Leaders of Character

It isn't how you look, where you work, what you have, who you know or what you know that counts. It is who you are when no one is looking. It's character that counts.

Real ministry is driven by men of character. One of my favorite passages on leadership is 1 Samuel 16:7. God tells

Samuel not to look at the outward appearance of a man, the things that people look at. God looks at the heart. What a key principle for selecting men to lead your ministry! Some additional helpful guidelines are the lists Paul gave to Timothy for selecting elders and deacons (1 Timothy 3:1–13). And 1 Timothy 4:12 makes one of the best measuring tools for choosing leaders. It provides five standards to measure a man's character:

Speech. Does he use his tongue to tear down or to build up? Does he lie or speak the truth? Is he sarcastic and cutting—or loving and kind?

Life. Is there consistency between his behavior on Sunday and Monday? Does he visualize what he verbalizes, behave in accordance with what he believes? There is no room on a leadership team for someone who isn't living faith in the marketplace.

Love. Is his heart interested in the well-being of others? Does he show compassion and tenderness toward others?

Faith. Is he willing to take wise risks and live on the edge? Is he willing to trust God—or does he live purely by human strength?

Purity. Is this man seeking to be morally, ethically and spiritually pure before God? That doesn't mean he's arrived—but is he striving to do right?

When Bill Clinton ran for president against George Bush he had a sign at his campaign headquarters that read, "It's the Economy, Stupid." His campaign team never wanted to lose sight of what they felt was most important. We need a sign in the front of our churches that says, "It's Character, Stupid." Remember what's most important when you select men to be on your leadership team.

Leaders Known for Godliness

The greatest gift your leadership team can give the men of your church is their personal holiness. There is nothing more important in leading other men to Christ than a vital, authentic relationship with Jesus. Men today want the real thing, not secondhand religion. They want reality, not more ritual. In selecting men to be on your team, start with men you know who are in love with Jesus. Some things I look for are:

Strong Private Life. Do they spend time with Jesus on a regular basis? When I get together with men I often ask them what they are learning in their daily devotions. A long stare after that question is a good clue there isn't much happening in that area of their life. Unless they drink from Jesus on a regular basis they will have nothing to give to others. What they are in private with Jesus will directly influence what they do in public with other men.

Obedience. Are they seeking to obey God in all areas of life or is there an area where they knowingly continue to sin? Are they open to accountability to others for their life and actions?

Worship. Godly men love to worship. They make sure they meet regularly with God's people to worship. If a man's hobbies, golf game or favorite spectator sport regularly cause him to miss Sunday worship, he's making a loud statement of his priorities.

In short, look for men whose lives point others to God rather than to themselves, who are becoming more and more like Jesus in all they say and do.

Leaders of Passion

Every once in a while when I least expect it I get a huge bear hug from John. After squeezing all the air out of me he says, "Steve, I just love working with men. I just wish I could do this full-time."

That is passion for ministry. To have a passion is to be enthusiastic about what you are doing, to not be able to wait until the next time you get together with your men. It's a love for what you are doing and a thankfulness that God has given you gifts and the incredible privilege of serving Him. When I interview men for leadership positions I ask a few questions that help me gauge their passion for ministry: What is your vision for men's ministry? What gets you the most excited about serving? Where do you see yourself fitting in? From these questions and others I can get a sense of whether they really want to do ministry, or if they are motivated by guilt or by a feeling they should just do something for the sake of doing something.

Gifted Leaders

The final quality I seek in a man for my leadership team is giftedness. Every man is gifted, but I want to make sure that a man is gifted for his area of responsibility.

Our natural tendency is to surround ourselves with men just like us—people we want as friends. Men with different gifts think differently. They might laugh at opposite things. They process experiences and emotions in a variety of ways. It can be death to a ministry if everyone on the team is the same. The Packers' head coach, Mike Holmgren, is a great offensive coordinator but is relatively weak on defense. So he surrounds himself with strong defensive minds, men who compliment his offensive schemes. In the same way, a leader of men needs to surround himself with other men who complement his giftedness.

As you pull together a group of men, think through the following areas to get a well-rounded team:

Is there someone with the gift of leadership? Many times people lead—even pastors—who do not have the gift of leadership. A leader has the ability to develop a vision and get others into it. They can mobilize others and get them involved in making that vision a reality. Every team needs one.

Is there a person with the gift of administration? A ministry start-up generates endless amounts of administrative tasks. Find someone who likes administration—keeping ministry details organized and workers on-task and on-time.

Any man with the adventurous spirit of a leader needs a guy like this.

Is there a person with the gift of helps? With so much to get done you need to have someone on the team who relishes doing the little things, the behind-the-scene things, that make a ministry work.

Is there a person with the gift of mercy? Sometimes a leadership team full of guys who like to get things done leaves a bunch of battered people in their wake. You need someone who can care for the men, be a kinder and gentler example to overeager leaders and shepherd the other leaders as the team develops.

That isn't a comprehensive list, but these four giftings are keys that keep a team working well. They bring balance to each other. It's possible, though, to have the proper gift mix but still get nowhere. These gifts are different enough that the team needs to work at working well. Each man must bring with him not just a gift but a deep willingness to be a team player.

As you pull together your coaching staff for your men's ministry, keep in mind the words of E. M. Bounds:

> God's plan is to make much of the man, far more of him than anything else, because men are God's method. The church is looking for better methods; God is looking for better men. The Holy Ghost does not flow through methods, but through men. He does not come on machines, but on men. He does not anoint plans, but men. It is not great talents nor great learning that God needs, but men great in holiness, great in faith, great in love, great in fidelity, great for God. Those men can mold a generation for God.[4]

As you build your leadership team you're seeking men who display servanthood, character, godliness, passion and giftedness. Work through Exercise 2 to see where your team is at right now.

Exercise 2—Us: On a Scale of 1 to 10

1. Each man on the team should take time to rank where he is in each of these areas.

	Excellent	Average	Needs Work
a. Servant Spirit	1 2 3 4	5 6 7	8 9 10
b. Character	1 2 3 4	5 6 7	8 9 10
c. Godliness	1 2 3 4	5 6 7	8 9 10
d. Passion	1 2 3 4	5 6 7	8 9 10
e. Giftedness	1 2 3 4	5 6 7	8 9 10

2. What are the strengths and weaknesses of our team right now? If there are four key gifts that we need—leadership, administration, helps, mercy—which gifts do we have? Which do we lack?

3. If you are a lone leader at this time, what type of men do you need to complement your gifts?

How to Recruit Your Coaching Staff

It's one thing to know what kind of person you want—even to set your sights on who you want. It's another thing to get him involved. If your church is like ours, 20% of the people do 80% of the work. All of the church's key people are pulled in many different directions. So when I started doing men's ministry a number of years ago I vowed I wouldn't steal leaders from another ministry. I would instead develop my own from the many who were on the outside looking in.

Here are steps you can take in recruiting men to be on your leadership team:

1. Pray Them Out. In Matthew 9:37–38, Jesus tells the disciples that the harvest is plentiful. That's true in our day as well. But what was the first thing He told them to do? Hire a headhunter? No! The first step is to pray to the Lord of the harvest to send workers for the harvest.

Someone shared this verse with me back in my seminary days. It has prompted me to keep a list of men in my journal who aren't currently involved in any ministry. Whenever I see someone at church that isn't involved—but who should be—I put his name on the list. I regularly pray through this list, asking God to thrust these people into the harvest, maybe in the men's ministry, maybe in another area. I pray that God would bring just the right position for this man, based on his giftedness, passion and availability.

Make a list. Start praying for men right now who can be part of your leadership team.

2. Develop Relationships With Them. One principle I will bang home throughout this book is that ministry happens best through friendships. Do things with potential leaders in order to know them. Take them out for breakfast or lunch. Within these informal settings you can begin to see where they are at.

3. Meet Them One-on-One. The best way to ask them to be involved is in one of those one-on-one settings. I usually meet them for a meal or in their office or my office. I try really hard to connect face-to-face before I settle for a phone conversation. To begin, I tell them that I have been praying about their involvement in the men's ministry and that I feel it's time to talk about a certain area. I then share our vision for the ministry and where we are going—the big picture. I work to recruit men to a vision, not a program. Once they grasp the big picture I share more specifically about the area I see them getting involved in. It could be heading up the small groups, or leading a small group, doing publicity for the ministry or a hundred other things. I let them know my perspective of why I think they are the right person for the job and how they would fit on the team.

4. Share a Job Description. At this one-on-one meeting I then share a straightforward job description for the specific area where I would like them to help. It helps to do this in writing to make everything as clear as possible, though you might choose to cover this verbally. The job description tells them specifically what I expect of them. It includes:

    a. What they would do—the ministry responsibilities.
    b. How much time it takes to do it.
    c. Who they report to.
    d. The term of service.
    e. What the men's ministry leadership team and the church will do to support them in their ministry.
    f. The qualifications necessary for the job.

After walking a guy through the job description I ask him if he has any questions about the ministry opportunity. (I have included a sample job description at the end of the chapter.)

5. Ask for a Commitment. I finish the conversation by asking my prospective leader to pray about the opportunity and, if he's married, to talk to his wife about it before making a commitment. I give him a specific time frame of when I need a response, usually a week to two weeks maximum.

These are the steps you could use in recruiting any leader for your ministry. Right now we are simply talking about getting your ministry started and all you are looking for is 3–5 men who will form your main ministry team. If there are two or three of you already, then you need to decide how many guys you want on your team and who should talk to who.

Exercise 3—Choosing Leaders

1. How many do you want on your ministry team? What types of men do you need on your team to bring a balance of gifts, personality, races and types of men? Ask God to help you think beyond your buddies to men who can broaden your ministry and genuinely help your efforts.

2. Make a list of men from your church that may be potentials for your Men's Ministry Leadership Team.
   (a)

   (b)

   (c)

   (d)

   (e)

3. After spending time in prayer about it, who do you want to ask to be a part of the team? Who is going to ask them?

The God Who Makes Things Happen

You need a point man to make things happen. Then you need additional men to form a leadership team to help him, because men's ministry isn't a one-man show. But you also need to move ahead certain that *God* is the supreme head over all you do. You can make your plans and ask God for His rubber-stamp approval. Or you can invite Him to guide and empower all that you do.

How do you know God is leading your ministry? Pray. It's the undergirding for the rest of your ministry. Ask God for His help. Express your dependence on Him. In prayer humbly invite God to act.

Before you flip to the next chapter to look for more "How-To's of Men's Ministry," consider these words of S. D. Gordon from his *Quiet Talks on Prayer:*

> You can do more than pray after you have prayed. But you cannot do more than pray until you have prayed. Prayer is striking the winning blow at the concealed enemy, service is gathering up the results of that blow among the men and women we see and touch.[5]

Once you have a leader in place who has a vision, passion, the giftedness and character to lead the ministry, and as you're starting to build your leadership core, your next step is to pray. For a ministry to move forward and bear lasting fruit it must move forward on its knees. Unfortunately, in many churches today prayer is only given lip service. We talk about it, we sing about it, we read about it, but rarely do we do it. Years ago I heard the story of Charles Spurgeon and his famous "Furnace Room of Prayer." The story goes like this:

> An American couple visiting England a number of years ago decided to take a tour of Charles Haddon Spurgeon's Baptist Tabernacle, one of the most famous

churches in London. Thousands came each week to hear Dr. Spurgeon, and every week scores were converted. The couple arrived at the church an hour before worship began, and as you might imagine, there was no one yet in the sanctuary. They looked around for a few minutes trying to figure out what to do, when a bearded gentleman came up to them and asked, "May I help you?"

"Yes. We're visiting from America," they explained, "and before the service starts we would like a tour of the church."

The man said, "Well, I'm a member of the church. I'd be glad to give you a tour."

They thought that would be wonderful, but the man offered something quite out of the ordinary. "The first thing I want to show you," he said, "is our furnace room." The couple took pains to be polite but they really didn't want to see the church's furnace room. But when in Rome . . .

So they followed the man down the winding stairs of the Victorian building to the basement, then to the sub-basement, the sub-sub-basement and the sub-sub-sub-basement. As they went deeper and deeper into the ground it got danker and danker and darker and darker.

The American couple protested. "Well, you know, you don't need to take us any farther," they said. "We know what a furnace room looks like."

But the man remained firm. He said, "No, no. It's very important that if you're going to come to our church that you see our furnace room." So down to the final sub-basement they went, into the coal room where coal was piled everywhere. It was, of course, how the church was heated. The man indicated a huge oak door, bound by iron clasps and iron handles, and said, "This is our furnace room."

And they said, "Well fine, thank you very much. Now, may we see the rest of the church?"

"No, no, you haven't been in the furnace room yet!"

"Well, we don't really want to go into the furnace room."

He insisted. "But you must."

They relented. The man opened the huge door and they looked into the massive room with its boilers and furnaces. To their surprise, the room was filled with hundreds of people on their knees, praying the hour before the service.

The couple looked at the bearded gentleman, then back at the hundreds of people praying on the floor. When they turned to him again, he smiled and said, "Well, I've had my little joke with you. Yes, I am a member of this church and, in fact, I'm the pastor. I'm Charles Spurgeon. People come from all over the world to this church to see what God is doing and He is doing incredible things, but they think it's because of me that God is doing all of this. I'm not the reason it is happening. The reason things are happening here is that every Sunday morning, from ten until noon, when I'm finished with the service, hundreds of people gather here in the furnace room. They pray for the service, for my sermon, for my ministry. They pray for conversions, for Christians to be fully committed to Christ. That is why God does the ministry He does at Baptist Tabernacle. It isn't because of me."

Every ministry needs a furnace room where men are committed to pray for both leaders and participants. The only way that I was willing to do men's ministry was if other men would pray for me and for the ministry on a regular basis. I found it vital to start a prayer ministry first. It's the place where the real work gets done. Five steps to making it work at your church:

Step One—Find a small group of men who will commit to pray regularly for you and the ministry. You can find these men through a number of means. You can make a list of 15–20 men and send them each a letter and a commitment card to return to you if they accept the challenge. You can run a bulletin announcement letting the men of your church know you are developing a prayer team.

I asked the men to pray and fast for the ministry every Wednesday noon. Some of the men had other meetings on Wednesday, so they had to do it another day. We didn't gather to pray; each man prayed on his own wherever he was. For an example of the type of commitment we ask for, look at end of the chapter for the "Frontlines Commitment Card" we had the men fill out.

Step Two—On a regular basis send the requests for your ministry out to the men. I send a prayer card before the first Wednesday of the month so the men can pray specifically. These cards usually have new requests, both personal and ministry, as well as answers to prayer. See "Frontlines Prayer Requests" card at the end of the chapter.

Step Three—Get the men together. During the course of the year we have a breakfast for the entire prayer team to come together. We get to know one another and have a couple guys share testimonies of how things are going. We talk about struggles as well as joys.

Step Four—Keep the men informed. This happens in two ways. First, I use a monthly newsletter to instruct the men on prayer. I encourage them to read and to be growing in prayer. One year we read through *What God Does When Men Pray*, by William Carr Peel (Colorado Springs, Colo.: NavPress, 1993). Another year we read *Too Busy Not to Pray*, by Bill Hybels (Downers Grove, Ill.: InterVarsity Press, 1988). This year they are reading *Revival Fire* by Wesley Duewel (Grand Rapids, Mich.: Zondervan Publishing House, 1995). The second way I keep them informed is to let them know how God is answering prayer. I did an awful job of this the first year. Men kept asking how my talks went. How the events went. They had prayed. They wanted to know if anything had happened. It told me that if I asked men to pray I had better watch for answers and pass them on to the men. There's no greater motivation for prayer than to see and hear about answers to prayer.

Exercise 4—Building a Prayer Team

1. Make a list of five men you could ask to be on your prayer team.

    (a)

    (b)

    (c)

    (d)

    (e)

2. What are you going to ask them to pray for?
    Personally
    (a)

    (b)

    (c)

    Ministry
    (a)

    (b)

    (c)

3. How are you going to keep these men growing in prayer and informed of answers to prayer?

As you begin to develop your leadership team I would suggest you find one person to be responsible for the prayer team. Our prayer coordinator collects all the requests and gets them to prayer team members. It takes the responsibility off you and helps another man to grow!

In the next chapter we will talk about "scouting." A team can't win if they don't know who they're working with. We will look at how to find out more about who men are and how to survey them to find out their needs, their visions and what they want from your men's ministry.

Other Resources for Prayer:

How to Develop a Prayer Partner Ministry, Injoy Ministry, 1530 Jamacha Road, Suite D, El Cajon, CA 92019. Phone: (619) 444–8400, 1–800–333–6506.

The Complete Works of E. M. Bounds on Prayer, Baker Book House, Grand Rapids, Mich., 1990.

Mighty Prevailing Prayer by Wesley Duewel, Zondervan Publishing House, Grand Rapids, Mich., 1990.

Churches That Pray, by Peter Wagner, Regal Books, Ventura, Calif., 1993.

Notes

1. Quoted by Ravi Zacharias from the book by Richard Elsworth Day, *Filled With the Spirit*, in a message given at the 1988 Elmbrook Missions Conference.
2. George Barna. *The Frog in the Kettle: What the Christian Community Needs to Know About Life in the Year 2000* (Ventura, Calif.: Regal Books, 1990), p. 148.
3. Henri Nouwen, *In the Name of Jesus: Reflections on Christian Leadership* (New York, N.Y.: Crossroads Publishing House, 1989), pp. 63–64.
4. E. M. Bounds, *The Power of Prayer* (Grand Rapids, Mich.: Baker Book House, 1972), p. 269.
5. S. D. Gordon, *Quiet Talks on Prayer* (Uhrichsville, Ohio: Barbour and Company, Inc., 1984), p. 16.

Elmbrook Church Men's Ministry
Job Description

Job Title: Top Gun Instructor

Reports to: Top Gun Coordinators

Ministry Responsibilities:
1. To go through the training program for TG instructors.
2. To prepare the lesson each week for the meeting.
3. To facilitate the discussion each week of the Bible study.
4. To meet with the men in an informal setting two–three times throughout the year.
5. To dialogue with the co-leaders on a regular basis regarding the well-being of the group and those in the group.
6. To participate in the services during the course of the year.
7. To pray on a regular basis for your group.

Length of Service: Nine-month commitment to the ministry. September is training and the groups run October–May.

Time Required: Average of four hours a week.

In-Service Support:
1. Training sessions before you start.
2. Periodic in-service meetings.
3. Shepherd from TG Leadership Team to pray for you on a regular basis and to be available to you at all times to talk.

Qualifications and Special Skills:
1. Elmbrook church member.
2. Must have gone through TG Basic Training.
3. We expect regular church attendance at Elmbrook.
4. We expect you to make your personal devotion time a priority.
5. We expect you to attend all training sessions.
6. We expect you to be prepared each session.

Prayer Requests

Top Gun
- For the men to connect into a plan of service following the Leadership Module.
- For the development of a business plan for Top Gun.
- For completion of the T. G. II curriculum: writing of the discipleship and mentoring lessons.

Breakfast of Champions at the Country Inn, Waukesh—April 20
- For Stuart and John Anderson as they prepare their talks and testimony.
- For the men of the church to have boldness in inviting friends to hear a clear Gospel presentation.
- That men would be drawn to Jesus.

General
- Wisdom in the development of the Small Group plan for the men.
- Praise for the great "No Regrets" Conference!
- Pray for the development of the Philippines Missions Team.
- Pray for the planning of the May 17 men's year-end celebration.
- Pray for "Acts of the Apostles," March 28–31.

Steve's Personal Requests
- Trying to regroup after a *very* busy and draining January/February (emotionally, physically and spiritually).
- Trying to get a visa for the ministry trip to Beirut this summer. Not an easy one.
- Preparation for a hectic April/May—lots of retreats and speaking engagements.
- Pray for our family as we vacation together on March 30–April 12.
- Consistency in spiritual disciplines.

ELMBROOK'S PRAYER MINISTRY FOR MEN

We are constantly on a stretch if not a strain, to devise new methods, new plans, new organizations to advance the church and secure enlargement and efficiency for the gospel.... Men are God's method. The Church is looking for better methods; God is looking for better men.... The Holy Ghost does not flow through methods, but through men. He does not come on machinery, but men. He does not anoint plans, but men—men of prayer.
—*E. M. Bounds* The Preacher and Prayer
(*now* Purpose in Prayer)

One of the greatest sins the church in America needs to confess is the sin of prayerlessness. What is needed for the church to get back on track is prayer. The Frontlines Ministry is a group of men who are dependent on God and express this dependence in a life of prayer, which will in turn effect change in themselves to be men of integrity in their home, church and workplace. We are looking for men who will commit to be men of prayer. The commitment is as follows:

• It is for one year.
• It is to pray every Wednesday noon (or another day of the week if necessary) wherever you are, for the Men's Ministry, its leaders and its purposes.
• To work through individually a selected book on prayer/worship and be prepared to share what God is teaching you in your study.
• Fasting is optional this year, but we think you will be too busy praying to eat.
• Participate in the various prayer retreats and meetings which will be scheduled throughout the coming year.

If you are willing to move the church ahead on your knees, sign the card and return it to Steve Sonderman at Elmbrook Church, 777 S. Barker Rd., Brookfield, 53045. When you sign up, we'll send you the first set of prayer requests, book syllabus and more information. If you have any questions, call Steve Sonderman or Tom Trepczyk.

COMMITMENT CARD

Name _____

Address _____

City _____ State _____ Zip _____

Signature _____

Scouting the Players

A few years ago Willow Creek senior pastor Bill Hybels made this clear-sighted remark: "In order to effectively minister to people in the '90s," he asserted, "we must not only be able to exegete the scriptures, but society."[1] Soon we will not only be done with the decade but we'll move on to a new millennium. The date doesn't matter: What is crucial is that you have to base your men's ministry on a clear understanding of the "society" you work with—the men you want to reach and their roles in this world.

It isn't enough to understand the Bible. God intends for His Word to connect with men's daily lives. That won't happen if the person doing the connecting doesn't know the men he is leading. Before you build a ministry to and for your men you need to know them.

Too often local fellowships copy programs from other churches in other cities, then act surprised when the latest, greatest failproof model meets little success. But churches are different. People are different. The men of each church have different interests, pressures, schedules, incomes and needs. They aren't likely to accept a ministry developed without their input, however well-intended their leaders are. That great theologian and international diplomat Bobby Knight, basketball coach at Indiana University, takes that foist-my-way-on-them approach. When a guy goes to play basketball for Coach Knight, there's only one way to play the game: Bobby Knight's way. Knight recruits young men to fit his mold, his style of play. When it comes to basketball, it's his way or the highway.

That doesn't fly in the church. Every group of people is different. They expect different ministries. And ministries for them must be developed with them in mind.

Getting to Know Your Men

I can't tell you everything about the men in your church. This chapter is going to give you tools to effectively find out who your men are and identify their needs. We will look at how to interview and survey your men and how to keep your pastor involved in the process. I will wrap up the chapter by looking at men's ten most common needs—some of the issues you will probably uncover in your surveying. But the information *you* gather will likely be the most valuable thing you bring to the next stage of building a men's ministry—developing a game plan, structuring a program to meet real needs.

With these general characteristics in mind and a head leader and leadership team of 3–5 men in place, your next step is to interview and survey the men of your church. Are you sitting down? This process can take three to six months, though it can happen a little faster. If that sounds like a time-consuming project, consider these benefits:

You discover the needs of the men in your church. This is the only way you can get an accurate picture of *your* men in *your* church.

You avoid striking off in a wrong direction—blazing a trail for your men to follow and seeing no one follow. Men's ministry isn't for the leaders. It's for the men. It's meant to meet their expressed needs and deeper needs that may go unsaid. Surveying your men avoids needless work. I have a close pastor friend who began his working life as a builder and contractor. One of his favorite sayings: "Measure once, cut twice. Measure twice, cut once."

You will give the men of your congregation ownership of the ministry. They get in on the ground floor because the ministry is being developed with their awareness and input.

You will grow interest in the upcoming ministry, using this lead time to build anticipation.

Choosing Men for One-on-One Interviews

I would suggest you start with individual interviews. Meeting one-on-one enables you and your team to target specific men in the church to spend time with. The one big thing to remember: to make these meetings productive you have to go as a listener. Don't go to share ideas *you* have.

How many men you meet with is far less important than *who* you meet with. I met with 60 men because our church is large and being the men's pastor is my full-time job. You probably won't be able to do that. Consider the size of your church, but figure that your leadership team will do well if they meet with 10–16 carefully chosen men. When you set up your schedule of who you want to meet with, you will want as much variety as possible. Keep the following categories in mind:

Married men and singles
Men in their twenties to men in their seventies
Men with children and men without children,
Men who are working and men who are retired
Professionals and nonprofessionals
Men who go on the road for work often and men who don't
Men who have been involved in men's ministry and men
    who haven't
Men of different races

Men interested in sports and active outings and men who
   aren't
New believers and mature believers
Men on the inside of your church and men on the periph-
   ery.

In other words, try to get a good cross section of the men
of your church. The natural tendency is to meet only with
those you know and feel comfortable with. You can avoid this
by setting up a grid with age and some of the key characteristics across the top, running names down the left-hand side.
Think through and mark which men fit which characteristics—it's a good visual way to ensure you get a mix of men
from your church.

Connecting With Your Men

Once your team develops a list, divide up the names, call
the men and make appointments with them. Schedule a time
to meet with your pastor as well—and check out the guidelines below. Here is a list of things to mention on the phone
to your men:

1. Explain what you are doing and promise to take only one
hour of their time. Schedule your meeting at a time and location good for them. Remember: they are doing you a favor.

2. Tell the men that being interviewed doesn't mean
they're making a commitment to the men's ministry. All you
want is their input.

3. When a man says his opinion isn't worth anything because he doesn't know much about men's ministry, tell him
that you don't either—and that being a male is the only qual-
ification he needs. Once I let the men know there were no stupid responses, I didn't have a single man tell me he didn't
want to do it.

Meeting With Your Men

When it comes time to meet with your men, keep these
things in mind:

1. Give the men a set of questions ahead of time so they can think about them.

2. Call a day ahead to confirm the meeting.

3. If you don't know the man you are interviewing, introduce yourself and explain once again what you are doing.

4. Get right into it. Guys like to get to the business at hand.

5. Listen, listen and listen. There's no substitute for listening to what a man is saying. Work at making him the expert on men.

6. Stick to your agenda. Be flexible enough to take the conversation in different directions if you need to, but try to cover the questions your team decided on. You can use Exercise 1 to develop the list of questions you want to cover in your time together.

7. Close by thanking the man you interview for his time, energy and input. Ask him if he would like to see the results of the survey when they are tabulated.

Exercise 1—Interviewing Your Men

1. Your questions will be different from the ones I used because your church, men, and culture are different. But consider these as starters and modify them as needed:

    (a) What has been your involvement in men's ministry in the past? What do you see as its strengths? What do you see as its weaknesses?

    (b) Describe what you think are men's needs today. What are their main stresses, anxieties and pressure points? What are four to five characteristics of men today? What are men's greatest needs today? What do men want?

    (c) How can the men's ministry minister to men at Elmbrook and outside of Elmbrook?

(d) Based on what you have told me about men today, what type of ministry will best do the following: evangelism, establishment, equipping.

(e) What are your visions for ministry here at Elmbrook?

2. What questions would be most helpful for you to ask a number of men in your church? What do you really want to know from them?

   (a)

   (b)

   (c)

   (d)

   (e)

   (f)

   (g)

   (h)

   (i)

   (j)

Getting More Information

Get together with your leadership team after the individual surveys are completed and tabulated. Ask yourself the following questions: What are some of the common themes? What are some of the common needs of men in our church? What type of ministries are they envisioning? What do we feel would be effective in ministering to them based on what we heard?

Based on what you now know, put together a survey for all the men of the church. This survey provides you with the opportunity to take the general ideas that came from the individual surveys and ask specific questions. If the men say they are very interested in being in small groups, for example, you can ask in the all-church survey, "When is the best time for small groups to meet?" "Where should they meet?" "What do you want to study?" "Are you willing to lead a group?" and, "Are you interested in being in a group?" Here are some ideas to keep in mind when you put together the survey:

1. Ask your pastor for permission to do the survey. Show him what you have done so far and explain why you want to survey all the men. Ask him if the survey could be done during the service or if he would rather have it done afterward.

2. Make sure the survey can be done in five minutes or less.

3. Design questions so they can be answered with a check mark.

4. Have a few men read the questionnaire to make sure the questions make sense. Is each of the questions helpful for the development of the ministry? You may not get to do another all-church survey for years, so get the information NOW.

5. Arrange with the ushers how the survey will be collected. If you put the survey in the Sunday bulletin, you might want to have a well-marked drop-off box at each exit of the sanctuary.

6. Prepare ahead of time how you will tabulate the results.

7. Let the men know the results. Put out a special flyer with

the results or even list some in the bulletin so the men get a sense of what happened with the results. At the end of this chapter, I have included the survey we used as well as a handout that presented our findings.

Surveying Other Churches

One last thing you can do to generate ideas is to contact other churches in your city, state or even across the country and find out what they are doing in men's ministry. I spent many hours on the phone talking to men already doing men's ministry in their church or through a parachurch organization. I asked *what* they were doing, *how* they were doing it and *why* they were doing it. The more people I talked to the more ideas I had for the variety of things we could do for our men.

There's a great shortcut that gets you a lot of information from many churches all at one time. More and more states are hosting training sessions sponsored by Promise Keepers or other organizations and these conferences are great places to network with other churches. As more and more churches are starting men's ministries networking is getting easier.

Involving Your Pastor

Because I have pastored for twelve years, I fully appreciate the love-hate relationship pastors have with new ministry ideas. Pastors are excited—*someone else is grabbing hold of ministry!* At our church we have seen that the best ministries are those started at the grassroots level. Pastors are also nervous: *where is this thing headed?* Pastors look at the big picture of the whole church and wonder what additional demands they will face to keep one more ministry going. They can also interpret a ministry start-up as a slam that they aren't doing an adequate job to meet the needs of the congregation. Here are some steps you can take to help the situation:

1. *Include your pastor.* Meet with your pastor early in the

process. Before you even get started make an appointment with him to share your vision and ideas. Ask if he has any plans for starting a men's ministry and what they are. Ask him when it would be a good time to get something started. You might hear that the church is already starting a couple of other ministries this year and that he wants you to wait a year. Accept that as time to build relationships with your men and to fine-tune your understanding of what the men need.

Your pastor may ask you to speak to the church board, or put you under the supervision of an elder or deacon. If he does, work hard to include that man in your planning in the same way you would include your pastor.

2. *Interview your pastor.* As I mentioned earlier, get together with him when you do your survey. The time I spent with our senior pastor and other associates was highly profitable and I am sure it will be for you as well.

3. *Inform your pastor.* Send copies of the minutes from your meetings as well as the results of the survey. It will keep him from feeling you are a loose cannon. Keep him involved in the process by scheduling your planning meetings when he can make it—*if* he wants to be there. Ask him if he wants to be there or just be kept informed. Don't pressure him to attend.

4. *Intercede for your pastor.* You can give your pastor no greater gift than your prayer support. A church in Madison, Wisconsin, has a group of men that meet in the pastor's office each Sunday morning to pray for the pastor before he goes into the pulpit. What an encouragement that must be! Call your pastor and ask him how you can pray for him and his family that week or month. Ask if you can pass on his prayer requests to your prayer team.

5. *Invite your pastor.* Make sure you invite him to the events you sponsor. Ask him to speak at some of your events as well. Pastors enjoy the opportunity to get out with the guys and talk with them, hang out with them and bring teaching. Don't take it personally, though, if your pastor doesn't show up for every event. He could easily be at meetings every eve-

ning of his life if he said yes to everything. He does have a family and he needs his down time too!

6. *Incourage your pastor.* (Sorry—I couldn't settle for five out of six "I" words.) Make sure the men of your church encourage him in the work he is already doing. Drop him a note or give him a call to let him know how much he means to you and the church. There is no greater feeling for a pastor than knowing the men of the church stand with him.

Drawing Some Conclusions

By this point you have the information you need to begin to pray over the results and discuss what type of ministry will best help the men of your church grow. You have interviewed a variety of men in your church. You have surveyed men in your church. And you have incorporated your pastor's goals and ideas. It's time to get your team together. Exercise 2 will take you through a series of questions designed to help you critically analyze the information you have gathered.

Exercise 2—Pulling It Together

1. After looking through the surveys, what are some of the major themes that stand out?

2. What are the top three expressed needs of the men in our church?
   (a)

(b)

(c)

3. If the biblical man is a man of intimacy, integrity, identity
   and influence, where do our men seem to be doing best?
   Where do they need the most help?

4. What are the top three practical issues our men want to
   learn about?
   (a)

   (b)

   (c)

5. What type of ministry is going on already? What are its
   strengths and weaknesses? Where are our men involved in
   the church?

6. What type of ministry do our men want (retreats, small
   groups, monthly large group, and so on)? How well do their
   desires match the hopes and expectations of our pastor and

other church leadership? If they are significantly different, how will they be reconciled?

Men's Unspoken Needs

Let's wrap up by looking at some of the key needs I find among men at my church and other churches. Since many of these are inner needs, they may get lost in concrete talk of life problems and potential ministry programs. They might help you put your finger on issues your own men leave unsaid or unclear.

David Letterman has made his "Top Ten" lists famous. Here's my own list of men's needs that will impact how we design our ministries. Unlike Dave, however, I don't claim that my list is in order. I think each point is vitally important. Nevertheless, I give you *The Top Ten Needs of Men in the '90s*.

1. *Men Need Action*. The male self-image is largely determined by what they do and what they accomplish. Their goal orientation pushes them to achieve things, to focus until the task is accomplished. I have found that men enjoy working on projects where the results are solid and tangible. Projects like collecting clothes for a church-run store in Romania or helping to rehab a house for Habitat for Humanity fit with how men are designed.

2. *Men Need Safety*. One rule of masculinity is "Thou shalt not show emotion." Men are rarely vulnerable with one another if you don't provide a safe environment for openness.

A key ingredient that makes this happen is a clear commitment to confidentiality. When I do the Milwaukee Brewers chapel services before their Sunday games I occasionally get to go into the locker room and talk with some of the guys. You can't miss a sign above the door on the way out. It reads, "What you see here and hear here stays here." That's safe advice for men's small groups as well. If you want to see men develop authentic relationships with other men they need time and safety to do it.

3. *Men Need to be Challenged*. When I surveyed our men before starting our ministry, one thing I heard over and over again was "I want to be challenged." Men grow up with challenges. In school it's the big exam. In athletics it's the big game. In the business world it's the big sale—or a takeover or a new product or a new venture. We make it too easy on men. We expect nothing of them. When I read the Gospels I see Jesus over and over again drawing a line in the sand and daring the disciples to meet Him on His side. It's no different today. Men aren't interested in a ministry that gets together to chew the fat. They want to be challenged to act, pray, behave and think in a way that glorifies God. I find it helpful to remind the men often what is at stake—that we are dealing with kingdom realities.

4. *Men Need to Get to the Point*. The Christian male wants to know what the program is all about. They don't want to spend time on fluff, trappings and extracurricular activity. This mindset will greatly impact what and how you do your ministry—from how you present your mission and vision to how you advertise to how you run small groups and large events. They want to know what two or three practical life-applications they can take away from their time together.

5. *Men Need to Win*. Almost all of us have grown up with pressure to win. We are taught to be independent. Self-sufficient. Failure isn't an option.

Men bring this competitive nature with them to church—and into your men's ministry. You have to plan challenging yet achievable goals. You need to kill quickly programs that aren't working. One mistake I made was asking men in one of our small group programs to do two hours of homework in preparation for class each week. After a few weeks a man wouldn't show up. I'd give him a call. What I discovered over and over was that the guy wasn't getting his homework done so he was afraid to show up at the meeting. He was afraid to admit to the other men that he had failed. His way of dealing with it was to not come. Never underestimate the power of this drive not to fail.

6. *Men Need to Dream.* Men grow up dreaming and scheming big. As you design your ministry, give the men a chance to be a part of the brainstorming process (still to come in Chapter 6). Allow them to think big and see themselves involved in something bigger than themselves. This need to dream should impact your informal times with the guys as well. Over breakfast or lunch I like to ask men what they have been dreaming lately—if they could do anything, what would they do. Men want to discuss their dreams and find ways to act upon them.

7. *Men Need Other Men Like Them.* Men like to hang out with men just like them. That isn't always the best thing in the world, but it's not a bad place to start. One church I have been working with found that the best way to reach doctors was to have a small group for doctors. They have reached lawyers by having a group of those in that field. (What a group that must have been!) They discovered that men naturally gravitate toward men facing the pressures they face and doing the same jobs they do. This flocking together of birds of a feather isn't always true, but keep it in mind.

For a couple of years we tried to form small groups around a leader, time and topic. We had mediocre results. It was a nightmare trying to place everyone in the right group at the right time and place. This past year we told the men to find two or three guys they enjoy hanging out with and to start a small group. It's worked much better.

8. *Men Need Help Working Around Daily Work.* Downsizing and takeovers are wearing out men and their families. Add to that emotional weariness the long, odd hours most men work. The result? How and when you do ministry with men will largely revolve around their lives at work.

The most precious commodity for men in the '90s is time. They don't have enough of it. How they divide it is crucial. As leaders you need to consider the competing time demands men face and be sensitive about how many meetings you have and how long they last. Look carefully at your yearly schedule to ensure you don't pull them away from home and work too much. Since some men start early in the morning and others work late, you need to offer activities at a variety of times to meet the needs of the men you work with.

9. *Men Need Healing.* Not many of the men you minister to go to work and hear what a great job they are doing. When they get home their kids don't usually say what a great dad they have and thank him for working all day long so they can have a roof over their head and food to eat. Later that evening their wives probably won't applaud their performance as a dad or a husband. No, most of the guys you work with will be rather discouraged about life. They need a refuge where they can heal and be encouraged in their roles as men, fathers, husbands and workers.

10. *Men Need Freedom.* Men who are taught from boyhood to win develop a fierce independence. I have already mentioned that men have difficulty forming friendships with other men. They would rather stand alone and fight alone than work together. Your ministry will work to pull men together at the same time they reflexively pull apart. Men need respect for their space.

These are a few needs to consider when you begin to design your ministry. Before we move on I would encourage you to work through the following exercise individually or with your ministry team.

Exercise 3—The Key Needs of Men

Take each of the ten key needs of men and discuss how they
impact how you design your ministry. You might want to take
other needs you found in your surveys and consider the same
two questions for each.

1. Men need action.
   How is this manifested in men?

   How does that impact the men's ministry you plan?

2. Men need safety.
   How is this manifested in men?

   How does that impact the men's ministry you plan?

3. Men need to be challenged.
   How is this manifested in men?

   How does that impact the men's ministry you plan?

4. Men need to get to the point.
   How is this manifested in men?

   How does that impact the men's ministry you plan?

5. Men need to win.
   How is this manifested in men?

How does that impact the men's ministry you plan?

6. Men need to dream.
   How is this manifested in men?

   How does that impact the men's ministry you plan?

7. Men need other men like them.
   How is this manifested in men?

   How does that impact the men's ministry you plan?

8. Men need help working around work time.
   How is this manifested in men?

   How does that impact the men's ministry you plan?

9. Men need healing.
   How is this manifested in men?

   How does that impact the men's ministry you plan?

10. Men need freedom.
    How is this manifested in men?

How does that impact the men's ministry you plan?

Putting It All Together

Interviewing, surveying, working with your pastor, discerning needs—it can all feel tedious. It's well worth the time and effort. For a sports team to be successful the coaching staff must spend hours and hours looking at game films and watching players in order to decide how best to attack game day. It's no different in the ministry. To have a successful ministry you must take time to know the men of your church *before* you worry about putting together ministry plans. In the next chapter we will look at the undergirding principles of effective men's ministry—the things that can and should happen—and then look at how you can turn what you have learned into an effective men's ministry.

Notes

1. Bill Hybels, speaking at the Willow Creek Leadership Conference, February 1986.

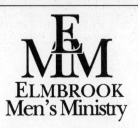

ELMBROOK
Men's Ministry

1992 SURVEY

THE MEN'S MINISTRY OF Elmbrook Church desires to help men be the men God created them to be. Take a few minutes of your time to help us plan and develop a ministry best suited to your needs. Please return this survey to an usher or to the Info Center, or by mail to: Elmbrook Church, Attention Steve Sonderman. Thank you for your time and input in this vital ministry.

Background Information
1. Age ❑ 18-24 ❑ 25-29 ❑ 30-39 ❑ 40-49 ❑ 50-64 ❑ 65 +
2. Marital Status: Single __ Married __ Number of Children ___
3. Type of work _____
4. Which of these issues are most important to you?
   (check two most important)
   a. ❑ Finding a Job   f. ❑ Parenting Skills
   b. ❑ Relationship to wife   g. ❑ Retirement
   c. ❑ Job security   h. ❑ Reaching other men
   d. ❑ Male roles and identity   i. ❑ Spiritual Life
   e. ❑ Balancing work, home and ministry

A Man and His Family
5. Would you be interested in a monthly meeting on family issues?
   (parenting, relationship to wife, etc.) ❑ Yes ❑ No

6. When would be the best time for you to attend that meeting?
   a. ❑ Saturday morning
   b. ❑ Weeknight   Which night? _____
   c. ❑ Sunday night
   d. ❑ Sunday morning

7. What topics would you like to see addressed? (check two)
   a. ❑ Keeping the romance alive in your marriage
   b. ❑ Disciplining your children
   c. ❑ Surviving the teenage years
   d. ❑ Being the spiritual leader at home
   e. ❑ Handling conflict
   f. ❑ Communicating with your wife
   g. ❑ Other_____

Men in the Marketplace

8. How can we best help you integrate your Christian faith into your job?
   a. ❑ Monthly meeting with a speaker
   b. ❑ Weekly small group meeting to discuss the issues
   c. ❑ Monthly small group meeting to discuss the issues
   d. ❑ 3-5 week seminar on ethics, relationships on the job, etc.

9. Best time for these small groups or seminars:
   a. ❑ Weekday morning
   b. ❑ Weekday evening
   c. ❑ Saturday morning
   d. ❑ Sunday evening

10. Topics I would like to hear addressed: (check top 3)
   a. ❑ Handling stress
   b. ❑ Changing careers
   c. ❑ Relationships on the job
   d. ❑ Sharing your faith with work associates
   e. ❑ Balancing home, work and ministry
   f. ❑ Keeping your ethic/edge sharp
   g. ❑ Coping with failure
   h. ❑ Mentoring
   i. ❑ Planning retirement
   j. ❑ Resisting sexual temptations
   k. ❑ Avoiding the success obsession

Men and the World

11. Would a short-term missions trip be of interest to you? ❑ Yes ❑ No

12. What type of short-term missions trip would interest you the most?
   a. ❑ Construction project
   b. ❑ Athletic trip (i.e. basketball in the Philippines)
   c. ❑ Business trip (i.e. giving seminars in Eastern Europe)
   d. ❑ Medical trip

13. What would be a good length of stay for such a trip?
   a. ❑ Weekend
   b. ❑ 1 week
   c. ❑ 2 weeks
   d. ❑ 3 weeks
   e. ❑ one month or more

Retreats

14. If we would begin to have retreats as part of the ministry, would you be interested? ❑ Yes ❑ No

15. What type of retreat would interest you most?
   a. ❑ Teaching type
   b. ❑ Adventurous type (canoeing, camping, fishing, etc.)
   c. ❑ Spiritual and personal renewal
   d. ❑ Networking with other men

16. And the length of the retreat?
    a. ❑ One night   b. ❑ Two nights

17. How far would you be willing to travel for a retreat?
    a. ❑ 30 minutes   d. ❑ 3 hours
    b. ❑ 1 hour   e. ❑ More than 3 hours
    c. ❑ 2 hours

Man to Man
18. Are you currently attending a men's Bible study group? ❑ Yes ❑ No

19. If you are not in a group, would you be interested in attending a men's small group? ❑ Yes ❑ No

20. What would you like to see happen in that group? (check two)
    a. ❑ Study the Bible
    b. ❑ Talk about problems at home and work
    c. ❑ Pray for one another
    d. ❑ Discuss how you integrate your Christian faith and your work and family life

21. Which would you prefer for meeting?
    a. ❑ Every week for one hour
    b. ❑ Once a month for three hours
    c. ❑ Every other week

22. When would you prefer to meet?
    a. ❑ Early morning before work
    b. ❑ After work in the evening
    c. ❑ Lunch hour
    d. ❑ Over the weekend

Men's Conference
23. What type of seminars would you like to see at the Men's Conference? (check three)
    a. ❑ Parenting
    b. ❑ Masculinity
    c. ❑ Relationship to wife
    d. ❑ Work ethics
    e. ❑ Changing jobs
    f. ❑ Dealing with retirement
    g. ❑ Balancing work, home and ministry
    h. ❑ Finances
    i. ❑ Evangelism
    j. ❑ Growing as a Christian
    k. ❑ Other _____

Men's Ministry

24. Would you be willing to assist in Elmbrook's Men Alive ministry?
    ❑ Yes   ❑ No

25. If yes, what are your areas of potential interest?
    a. ❑ Publicity
    b. ❑ Organize events (retreats, golf outings, etc.)
    c. ❑ Work in the kitchen
    d. ❑ Lead small group
    e. ❑ Do telephoning
    f. ❑ Work with work projects
    g. ❑ Marketplace Ministries

26. What do you or would you personally like to accomplish through
    your involvement in Men's Ministry? (check two)
    a. ❑ A closer walk with God
    b. ❑ Fellowship with other Christian men
    c. ❑ An outlet to vent problems or frustrations
    d. ❑ More involvement in the church
    e. ❑ A chance to meet other men
    f. ❑ Other (please specify): _____

27. When the entire men's program is determined, I would like someone
    to contact me so I can become more involved or receive more information.
    ❑ Yes   If yes, Name _____
             Phone # Days _____
             Eves _____
             Address _____
             City _____ Zip _____

    ❑ No

Please list additional comments about the Men's Ministry you may have in
the space below. You may optionally include you name, mailing address
and telephone number. Thank you very much for completing this survey.

Men's Ministry Survey Results
=Quick Facts=

What Issues Are Most Important to You?

1. Spiritual life
2. Balancing work, home and family
3. Relationship to wife

A Man and His Family

Would you be interested in a monthly meeting on family issues?
Survey says: Overwhelmingly "YES"

Men in the Marketplace

How can we help you integrate your Christian faith into your job?

1. Monthly meeting with a speaker
2. Monthly small groups to discuss the issue

What topics would you like to hear addressed?

1. Balancing home, work and ministry
2. Sharing your faith with associates
3. Keeping your ethical edge sharp

Men and the World

Would a short-term missions trip interest you?
Survey says: 60% "YES"

Retreats

If we held retreats as part of the Men's Ministry, would you be interested?
Survey says: 75% "YES"

Small Groups

If you are not already in a small group, would you be interested in one?
Survey says: 55% "YES"

I want to thank every man who helped by filling out a survey. The results will be very useful in planning the full program. I look forward to ministering with you in the coming years.

Steve Sonderman
Associate Pastor—Men's Ministry

Dreaming of the Big Win

After a particularly disappointing midseason loss to a team the Packers were heavily favored to win, Coach Lombardi gathered his players in the locker room. It was deathly quiet as the players realized they were about to receive another tongue-lashing from their coach. Lombardi slowly turned to face the team. In a stern voice he said, "Men, in all my days of coaching and playing I have never witnessed such a poor exhibition of football. We did not tackle, run, throw or catch the way you have been taught. Starting right now we are going to begin with the basics." With that he pulled out a football and held it in front of them. "Men," he said, "this is a football."

After a couple of seconds of silence, all-pro middle linebacker Ray Nitschke raised his hand. "Coach," he said, "could you go a little slower?"

Sometimes I feel like Lombardi. In men's ministry it's easy to get caught up in a thousand plans and plays and fine moves and to neglect the basics. We have already looked at who men are in the '90s and at the biblical man—the guy we are aiming to develop. We talked about recruiting a leadership team and together finding out what your men need and want. In Chapter 6 and beyond we will draw up and implement plans for ministry. But before we do that, I want to hold up the ball and say "This is a football." I want to work through the basic principles of an effective men's ministry, some of the things that can and should happen.

No matter what your ministry ends up looking like, no matter what the size or location of your church, there are principles that apply across the board. You want to develop a principle-centered, purpose-driven ministry, one that avoids weaving to and fro with every fad that hits the church or men's movement. You will gain benchmarks to measure all you are doing. And you will be able to ask yourself as a leadership team whether or not you are accomplishing your goals.

Principle 1: A Life-Changing Ministry Is Relationally Driven

Ministry happens best in the context of friendships.

As we have grown our ministry we have had to battle to stay people-centered rather than program-driven. Energy and excitement and numerical growth push any ministry to spin out another program, to devise another string of events. You need programs. But you also need to guard against letting planning and executing programs become so consuming that it robs time from building relationships. Authentic ministry happens when one man gets close to another man and develops a relationship with him. It's impossible to do ministry from a distance.

Some of you may have been thinking your church is too small to have a real men's ministry. Or you may have no pastoral oversight. Or you honestly don't see a lot of men in your church interested right now. Those are valid concerns. But you can still do men's ministry because it is rooted in relationships. Those can happen anywhere! Even if you're the only man in your church trying to make a difference you can have an informal but effective ministry simply by building relationships with the men of your church. All it takes is time and a listening ear.

The model for this up-close-and-personal ministry is Jesus himself. It tells us in John 1:14, "The Word became flesh and made his dwelling among us. We have seen his glory, the glory of the One and Only, who came from the Father, full of grace and truth." This is the Incarnation. He became man and "pitched his tent" among us. He left the splendor and majesty of heaven to live among sinful man. He left an unimaginably blissful comfort zone to show us how to live and die.

A recent article in *Christianity Today* recounted the faithful and effective ministry of Richard Halverson as chaplain of the United States Senate. "When one might expect to see the chaplain only on the Senate floor for the morning prayer, his presence is everywhere," Senator Hatfield stated. Halverson brought with him a lesson he had learned years earlier about the importance of simply being available to people at their convenience and in their time of need. In his book *The Living Body*, Halverson recalls that as a young minister he asked God to direct him to people in his congregation he should work to befriend. He felt God's Spirit lead him to contact a dentist he had seen in the pews. The dentist invited him to lunch. The dentist was shocked to reach the end of their time together to find that the pastor had no hidden agenda and wanted no money for the church but simply wanted to get to know him.[1]

What an incredible ministry you can have by building relationships with men in your sphere of influence, both believer and non-believer. I cannot tell you how many times this no-frills approach has opened doors for me to minister. I call a man and ask him to meet for breakfast or lunch—most of my meetings involve food. His inevitable first question: *Why?* What did I do wrong? What do you want? Where do you want me to serve? What are you trying to recruit me to do? I answer that I just want to talk and have a chance to get to know each other. They can hardly believe it!

Here are some basic guidelines you can use to build relationships with men:

1. *Walk with them.* One of the older and wiser associates on our staff gave me some advice when I started working with the men. He said, "Steve, when you meet with men, it is on their time schedule, their turf and their agenda." You build relationships with men by showing up in their world and walking with them. Go to where they live and work and see firsthand what their life is like.

2. *Listen to them.* When I meet I talk news, sports and weather for a while, then move on to some deeper, more personal questions like:

How are things between you and your wife?

How are things between you and your kids?

How are things between you and your job?

How are things between you and your Lord?

I rarely get through all of these because the talk usually flows into many related issues. My main goal in all of this is to work hard at just listening to what the man is going through in life. If he asks for advice I give it, if I have any. More often, though, I just allow him to speak. Many times small talk gradually leads to more significant talk.

3. *Love them.* John 13:34–35 says we are to love one another just as Christ loved us. Men today are starved for love and encouragement. The old adage is true: "People do not care how much you know until they know how much you care." People aren't going to be impressed by all the theology you know or what great programs you run. What stands out is your love and concern for them. So during these meetings I look for practical ways we can be helping in men's lives. I work to encourage them in how they are parenting, serving at church or seeking to live as a Christian in the marketplace.

4. *Pray for them.* I end our time together by asking the man how I can pray for him in the coming weeks. Sometimes it's appropriate to pray for him right there. If not, I promise to pray for him when I get back to the office.

Whether you have a church of 50 or 5,000, men's ministry starts with relationships. Taking time to develop friendships with men in the church is the best type of ministry you can have.

Exercise 1—Relationally Driven Ministry

1. What are some of the barriers to developing relationships with other men?

   (a)

   (b)

   (c)

   (d)

2. What can you as a leadership team do to ensure that your ministry is built—and continues to be built—on relationships?

3. What are some things you can do to build relationships—formally and informally—with the men of your church?

Principle 2: A Life-Changing Ministry Is Done by the Men Themselves

Two years after I became a Christian I was thrown into my first ministry opportunity. I was in college, and I was asked to lead a Bible study for students from the high school I had graduated from. When I arrived the first night there were thirty students waiting for me in the basement of one of the student's homes. I began by asking my students what they wanted to do on Wednesday evenings. They said they wanted a meeting where they would feel comfortable bringing their friends. They wanted to reach their school.

I told them I could never pull that off by myself. We started to divide up tasks. Treats—eats are important for high school ministry. Slide shows to illustrate my talk. Greeters. Musicians. Discussion group leaders. Before we left that first evening everyone in the room had an assignment for the next week. They not only knew they were into something much bigger than themselves but they felt important—everyone was vital to the ministry. The results were staggering. This small group of thirty students quickly grew to over 150 within a couple of years. I had been taught a major lesson in ministry. The church works best when everyone does his or her part.

Men's ministry is effective when it is done by the men themselves. Ephesians 4:11–12 states the principle: We are "to prepare God's people for works of service. . . ." The word "prepare" means "to set a broken bone," "to mend a frayed fishing net," "to restore something to its original condition" or "to condition an athlete." The only way a church will come to maturity, Paul says, is if people are deployed into service.

The first Reformation put the *Word of God* into the hands of God's people. Today we are in the middle of a second reformation that is putting the *work of God* into the hands of God's people. For many years most men have settled for ushering and maintaining church buildings and grounds. Men can do so much more. You will severely hinder your ministry's development if you try to do everything yourself. The task of the leadership is to give away the ministry to other men. Always be looking for men who can take responsibility. Again, to use the illustration of a coach: It isn't your job to play the game. It's your job to prepare your players to play. You train them. You develop their skills. You motivate them to work hard. In the same way the job of your leadership team is to train, develop and motivate men to serve both inside and outside the church. The principle I have tried to lead by is this: your ministry will only grow as fast as leadership is developed.

A couple of questions to ask yourself:

What am I doing that someone else could be doing? Maybe someone else can do it better. Maybe they can't. Give the job away and give a man a chance to learn. As our senior pastor says, "Anything worth doing is worth doing badly."

Which men aren't serving in the church who should be serving? I am not interested in stealing men away from serving somewhere else and signing them up to serve in my ministry. I look for guys sitting on the sideline who need a little encouragement to get into the game.

And some thoughts to keep in mind:

Don't start a new ministry until you have a leader lined up. It's easy to dream up great programs you could start for the men. But without leadership recruited and ready the job will fall back to you and your leadership team. If someone has a great idea for men, I listen. And then encourage *him* to start it. I provide support, training and prayer. I won't do what another man can do. God seems to work this way: If He gives a man the vision, then He's probably giving him the ministry.

Make service opportunities known. Just this month we were wondering who could organize our men going to the upcoming Promise Keepers Conference. Finally we listed our need in the bulletin. Five men showed up to be on the com-

mittee. If we hadn't made the job known we would still be ag-
onizing over who to ask rather than letting men's God-given
interests guide them.

*Start your ministry right by giving it away from the begin-
ning.* Your leadership team has to make widespread involvement in doing ministry a core value right from the start. It's
easier to talk about Ephesians 4 than to actually do it. It may
be hard for some on your team. They worry the job won't be
done well. They're probably right that it's easier to do it themselves. That isn't the point. Constantly ask your leaders who
they are getting to help them on whatever project they do.

Exercise 2—Ministry by Men

1. As a leadership team, make a list of the benefits of having
   a ministry where men actively serve.
   (a)

   (b)

   (c)

   (d)

   (e)

2. Make a list of places within your ministry where you need
   men to help right now (examples: men to collate surveys,
   handle publicity, staff registration tables, lead small
   groups, organize a retreat, etc.).

3. If your ministry is already up and running, where could you open up more places for men to serve?

4. Make a list of potential men from your church who could serve in your ministry.

Principle 3: A Life-Changing Ministry Shows Balance

During my years as a college pastor I worked with a variety of campus ministries. I was able to speak throughout the state at many of their groups. After a while it became obvious that each parachurch group had a hot button. For one group it was evangelism, for another it was small groups, for another discipleship and building up believers, and for yet another it was world missions. Each emphasis is good. Each is necessary. But each emphasis is just that—an emphasis. It can't be the whole picture.

It's easy to grow a ministry that gets so caught up in one biblical mandate that you ignore the others. The men of your church become muscle-bound in one area and 98-pound weaklings in another. It is possible, for example, to pour a great deal of energy, money and time into seeing unbelievers come to know Christ but then to spend little time grounding them in the basics and helping them become fully devoted followers of Jesus. Your attendance will be great but your men's maturity level dismal. It's possible, on the other hand, to spend so much time perfecting your care for one another that you never bother to reach out to those outside the faith.

The practical point is this: when you start to develop your ministry you want to plan a balanced ministry. I will be candid—this isn't easy. The trend today even in whole churches is to move toward one area or another.

When you develop your plan, keep these four biblical mandates in mind. I'm not saying that you will be able to address each of these the day you start your ministry. These are, rather, things to aim at as you move ahead.

Evangelism

In Mark 16:15 Jesus gave His disciples the mandate to go into the world and preach the Good News. Archbishop William Temple has a great definition of what Jesus meant. He says, "Evangelism is to present Jesus Christ in the power of the Holy Spirit, that men come to put their trust in God through Him, to accept Him as their Savior and to serve Him as their King in the fellowship of His church."[2]

There are more than three billion people on earth who don't know Jesus Christ as Lord and Savior. Most of the men you have in your ministry are surrounded on a daily basis by people who make up this category. Part of your ministry needs to be designed for those in your community who are without God, without Christ, without hope. Here are a few brief principles that will help you develop a ministry that reaches out to non-Christian men:

See evangelism as a process. Many people see evangelism as a Tuesday night mugging session. There's a reaping mentality that says you have blown your job if men at your meetings don't immediately pray a prayer to accept Christ. But in John 4:34–37, Jesus likens evangelism to farming. Some dig up the hard ground, others plant the seeds, still others water and weed and in the end someone gets to harvest the crop. Evangelism is the same way. You make your presence known in the community through lives that are pure, holy and loving. You proclaim the Gospel in verbal witness. In time you help non-believers step over from a life separated from Christ to a new life with Christ.

Think beyond the walls of the church. The average believer loses contact with all of his non-Christian friends within two years of becoming a Christian. Encourage your men to see their sphere of influence as the places they spend most of their time—likely their workplace and neighborhood. A survey conducted in Chicago's downtown loop asked 400 business people who they would most likely talk to about spiritual things. Given four options—a priest, an evangelist, a family member or the person working in the office next to theirs—more than 90 percent said the person working in the next office. That person would best understand their stresses. You can help your men see the need to develop relationships with those right around them.

Supplement their personal evangelistic efforts. While your men are busy building bridges with those around them, start to plan activities throughout the year that supplement their efforts. Plan events designed for men to bring other men. Each spring, for example, we do a "Breakfast of Champions" at a local hotel. The meeting is short and sweet, with a testimony and message tailored to the seekers in the audience, who have been personally invited by the men of the church. We even tell our men not to come if they don't bring a guest, because the event has one purpose—to proclaim the message of Jesus. As a leadership team, think hard about what you can do that is specifically evangelistic.

Train your men. Most men haven't been trained in one-on-one evangelism. Not only are most men unsure how to explain their faith point by point to another man, most men aren't able to share their own testimony with another man. Build into your ministry events that aim to teach all the men in your church to share the Gospel. You could accomplish your goal through a special Sunday school series. We include it in our

"Top Gun" program, which I will describe later in the book. Bill Hybels' book *Becoming a Contagious Christian*[3] is an excellent text, as is Paul Little's book *How to Give Away Your Faith.*[4]

Establishment

Men need not only to commit their lives to Christ but to be grounded in that relationship. In Colossians 2:6–7 Paul writes, "Just as you received Christ Jesus as Lord, continue to live in him, rooted and built up in him, strengthened in the faith as you were taught, and overflowing with thankfulness."

Most men aren't well grounded in the basics of Christianity even after years of church involvement. They can say and do the right things, but they have little vitality in their relationship with Jesus Christ. In the "establishment" area of your ministry you can help men to be what they have positionally already become in Christ. It's a process of grounding them in the basic spiritual disciplines of prayer, Bible study, solitude and memorization. It's here where you give them skills to walk with Jesus the rest of their lives, so they aren't dependent on others for their growth. It's here where they learn what it means to be a disciple of Christ—to obey Him, learn of Him, follow Him and become like Him. Some principles to keep in mind for this area of your ministry:

Use natural bridges. If one of the men in your church leads another man to Christ, he may be the best person to do the follow-up work. He could use a tool like the Navigator's *Operation Timothy* and meet with the man for several weeks to cover the material.

Use small groups to build men. Later we will spend a whole chapter talking about how to develop a network of small groups in your ministry. For now let's just say that small groups are an unbeatable way for men to grow in their relationship with Jesus. Small groups are places where men are encouraged, challenged, prayed for and held accountable. It's where the flames of faith can be fanned. As a leadership team, ask yourself how you can get small groups going in your church.

Don't overlook the basics. With the wealth of men's material on the market today, it's easy to study topics like parenting, being a better husband or getting along at work—and never deal with the issue of Christian growth. Keep in mind that your goal isn't just to mold men into better dads and husbands. You want men to learn to love Jesus Christ and obey Him in every area of life. The recent men's movement is compartmentalizing men—even despiritualizing them. It isn't a good trend. Within your curriculum for both small groups and large groups you want to include material that grounds men in the basics of Christianity as well as in men's issues.

Equipping

You don't want to raise a bunch of human sponges who attend your meetings solely to take in what they can. The third part of a balanced ministry is getting men out of the stands and into the game. Help your men discover, develop and deploy their spiritual gifts. Help them highlight areas in the church where they can serve. Help them not only to understand but also to practice good stewardship of time, energy and money. In short, help them become contributing members of the body. Some principles to keep in mind:

Provide ongoing training. As with evangelism, most men haven't had teaching in the area of spiritual gifts and servanthood. This is something you can build right into your small group curriculum if it isn't offered on a churchwide basis. Christian bookstores have many gift assessment books; one we have found helpful is *The Willow Creek Assessments.* A new tool that looks in depth at how talents, spiritual gifts, values, passions, and personality fit together is *LifeKeys* from Bethany House Publishers.

It's important when you use gift assessments to talk with each class participant to discuss what they found and where they want to serve. The crucial point is to connect them with service opportunities—and to let them try something else if their first shot isn't a good fit.

Pair men with mentors. Most men prefer to learn by watching and doing rather than sitting in never-ending classes. Keep *all* your training opportunities active and practical. Give special attention, though, to pairing new men with experienced leaders in your church. Whatever the ministry skill to be learned, the time is both educational and encouraging.

Form men in teams. Throughout our church we have groups of friends that serve together. Some areas of our youth Sunday school, for example, are run by teams of singles or young marrieds. Other classes are taught by pairs and trios of men. Give your men away and let them impact your church *together.*

Sent Out

Mission is the final piece of a balanced ministry. Nothing is more exciting than to see men involved in Christian Businessmen's Committee (CBMC) or prison ministry or sports ministries or missions. The fact that the church exists to take the whole Gospel to the whole world is something to continually keep in front of your men. Around our place we call it becoming a "World-class Christian." One criteria you can use down the road to evaluate your ministry is how many men you train and send to serve in ministries that reach non-Christians. Keep in mind the following:

Encourage "vacations with a purpose." These two-day to two-week trips allow men to experience a culture different from their own. Your men can take a construction trip, business trip, prayer trip, sports trip or medical trip. Whatever their task it's a great way to expose your men to what God is doing around the world. Pre-trip training and the trip itself teach the men what missions is all about.

Men who have gone on our trips to the Philippines, Romania or South America have all said that the trip was instrumental in their growth as a Christian and in their involvement in world missions. They come home knowing that "We are to be global Christians, with a global vision because our God is a global God," as John Stott puts it.[5] Mission trips are another chance to help men realize they are part of something enormously bigger than themselves—that they can help every nation, tribe and people come to know Jesus. In a later chapter I will discuss how to plan and carry out a short-term mission trip with your men.

Profile missions in your ministry. Because some men aren't anywhere close to going on a cross-cultural trip you need to bring missions to them. You can have missionaries on furlough share at your large group meetings. You can spend time praying for the missionaries your church supports. During our annual churchwide missions fest we throw a special men's breakfast for all the visiting missionaries. They get to eat with the men and share what they are doing and tell how the men can pray for them. It's a highlight of our year. You can also feature at your meetings men getting ready to leave on short-term trips. Have them explain what they will be doing, why they are going and how the men can pray for them. All of these things build excitement for world missions.

Include missionaries in your ministry. When missionaries are home on furlough they need places where they feel encouraged and loved. Ask your pastor if there are any missionaries in the area that you can invite to join a small group—not to lead but to simply be one of the guys. It's an excellent way you can minister to them.

Highlight parachurch ministries. Many wonderful ministries need your men. Periodically you can feature one of these ministries not only to let the men know what the group does but to advertise ministry opportunities. You could feature ministries such as the Gideons, Athletes in Action, Fellowship of Christian Athletes, Prison Fellowship or the Christian Businessmen's Association. These are all worthwhile ministries as are hundreds of others.

It could be easy to be overwhelmed as you read through these four keys to a balanced ministry. Let me say it again: these won't all be in place from the beginning. You need to go slow to develop a solid foundation. But as you grow, keep these four areas in mind so as to develop a balanced ministry.

Exercise 3—Balanced Ministry

1. As you have grown in your relationship to the Lord, which of these four mandates do you naturally migrate toward?
   - Evangelism
   - Establishment
   - Equipping
   - Sending

2. In developing a men's ministry, what are some steps you can take to keep your ministry balanced?

   If you have a ministry already:

3. How do you see each of the above four components represented in your ministry?

4. What "bridges" have you put in place to move men along? How well are your own men using these?

5. What are you doing that is different from what you originally set out to do? Have you been sidetracked?

6. Take time as a leadership team to brainstorm on what you could do under each of the aforementioned four areas in your ministry.

Principle 4: A Life-Changing Ministry Happens in Manageable Pieces

Leading men has as much to do with *how* we do ministry as *what* we do. The good news is that when you read through the New Testament—and more specifically, through the book of Acts—there isn't one "right" way to do ministry. It doesn't say anywhere that when you have a men's ministry you have to do these specific things. What we see instead are principles that span the ages, principles still relevant to how we do ministry today. In this last section we will look at a number of basic principles to keep in mind as your leadership team shapes how you will do ministry in your specific setting. The key question you want to ask yourself is this: *How* are we going to reach the goals and objectives we have set for our ministry? The funnel diagram on the next page, for example, shows how *we* work to move men to maturity. It gives these principles a

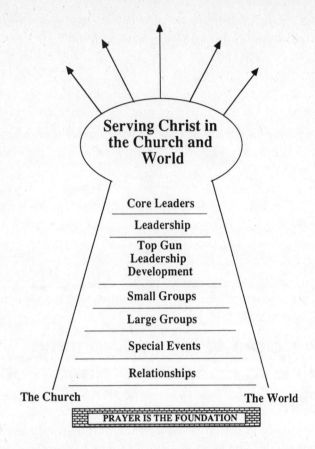

Serving Christ in
the Church and
World

Core Leaders

Leadership

Top Gun
Leadership
Development

Small Groups

Large Groups

Special Events

Relationships

The Church   The World

PRAYER IS THE FOUNDATION

shape. It suggests how programs accomplish goals.

Principle 1: *Start Ministry With Relationships.* We have already discussed this point at length, but remember that all effective ministry starts with men building bridges with other men within their sphere of influence.

Principle 2: *Make Ministry a Progression.* If faith is a process of growing into Christlikeness, then ministry should likewise be a *process* of growing men. Men's ministry isn't an isolated event, but an intentional series of steps that help men become fully devoted followers of Jesus. It's easy to fall into the trap of providing any number of unrelated activities for the guys at your church. Whenever you plan an event or a new ministry, ask yourself how it fits into your philosophy and purpose. Does it help you reach your goals and objectives—or just take up time and energy?

Principle 3: *Provide a Variety of Entry Points.* Small things can make it difficult for men to become a part of your ministry. A number of years ago part of our college ministry met at a home on a Monday evening. When our leadership team thought about the situation we realized we were making joining the study unnecessarily hard. The home was in an out-of-the-way neighborhood and hard to find at night. Parking was difficult. And students had to walk up to a stranger's house all alone. Not an optimal arrangement to make the first step easy. Don't count on your men being any more brave or persistent than my college students. Work hard to spot a variety of hassles: out-of-the-way meeting places, inconvenient times, awkward first moments, lack of opportunities to mix and become part of the established group.

Ask yourselves not only how hard it is to get involved but how many entry points you have created. Different men are attracted to different things. Some want sports. Some like speakers. Some hate to sing. Others love it. Some like large groups. Others prefer small groups. You won't be able to provide a lot of options all at once, but as you grow make sure you create a good mix.

Principle 4: *Blaze a Path for Growing Commitment.* As you move up the funnel the level of commitment increases. All it takes for a man to take part in our special events is for him to show up and listen. At our monthly large groups they come, listen and discuss the material presented—but not at a deep personal level. In our small groups there is minimal homework but the sharing goes deeper. Men at the Top Gun level meet many more expectations.

As you plan your program, ask whether or not you are making opportunities for the men to grow in commitment. Make the next step clear—not to exclude anyone, but to tap into men's love of challenge. Again, when you start you won't be able to provide the full range of commitment levels. When we began, for example, we had a shortage of leadership. We started with Top Gun groups, with the specific goal of developing leadership for the ministry. A couple of years later we were able to backtrack and add some of the less demanding ministries.

Principle 5: *Root Your Ministry in Culture.* Like every community and city, every church is different. Don't take a model from another place and spring it on your church! Pay attention to your surveys and the characteristics of your men and your church. Those are the factors that weigh heavily in deciding how to minister to your men. Fight the temptation to be like everyone else.

Principle 6: *Take Time to Build.* I need to say it again: Move slowly! If you want to build a ministry with staying power, take your time. We want everything now. The current enthusiasm for men's ministry creates a temptation to do events for the sake of events. But real ministry will attract men anytime. I can't bang the drum any louder. Don't hurry.

Principle 7: *Decentralize.* Women seem to have a herding instinct that makes them want to gather in large groups all the time. I have found that men's ministry happens best out where men are at—on their own turf. While you will need to do some ministry at your church, like monthly or quarterly breakfasts or meetings, most of what you do happens best in homes and in the marketplace. Moving out of the church helps men realize the church isn't a building but a group of people that cares for one another. As you measure your ministry, look at how much is church-based and how much is marketplace-based.

Principle 8: *Open a Variety of Service Opportunities.* In the same way that you need several points for the men of your church to enter your ministry, so you will want to develop a number of ways for men to serve. Some service options make minimal demands. Others carry a much greater commitment.

Not only is there a variety of commitment levels to accommodate, but also a variety of gifts. Each man is gifted and has a place where he uniquely fits. List ways men could serve and make that list available to your men. Try not to stereotype or pigeonhole men into just a couple of traditional service options. Notice that the funnel is open-ended. A funnel isn't designed to hold water, but rather to channel it in the right direction. The same with ministry. It shouldn't be designed to trap men but to train, equip, mobilize and send them out into the church and the world.

Principle 9: *Take Advantage of Affinity Groups.* A hot trend in reaching non-Christians today is "affinity group evangelism." It says that lawyers are most likely to reach lawyers, teachers best able to reach teachers. God wants us to reach beyond our comfortable boundaries, but affinity group evangelism recognizes that reaping is often easiest among people with shared concerns. As you strategize, think about how this principle might influence small groups and evangelism—who is in them and where they meet. You might want, for example, to have a small group for doctors. They are on similar schedules—crazy—and they face similar pressures. By being in a small group together they can share their stresses and shepherd younger doctors just entering the fray. This of course applies to any occupation.

Principle 10: *Get Excited About Church-Based Ministry.* Parachurch groups like Promise Keepers, The Gathering and CBMC are all significantly impacting our country today. I am grateful to be able, for example, to take our men to the PK summer conferences. It's one of our many special events during the year. But from talking with PK leaders I know they want their organization and events to be used as a *resource*, not as a *replacement* for the week-in, week-out ministry that happens in local churches.

It's easy for men to get excited about parachurch groups. Parachurch organizations don't carry all the baggage a church does. They are usually tightly focused on one goal—such as missions or reaching men or college students. They often

choose to deal with only certain types of people—and leave
the misfits and the hurting behind. What the church may lack
in the lean-and-strong feel of the parachurch, however, we
make up for in the diversity of God's body. We stand together
as God's community on earth, often as witnesses to His power
in weakness. For all these reasons I would strongly suggest
you keep your ministry church-based, aiming to in some way
impact all the men of your church.

Principle 11: *Center on the Word of God.* Last—and most
important—give your men the gift of the life-changing Word
of God. It's God's revelation of himself. It sets forth His guidelines for living. As I tell our guys, it's their playbook for life at
work, home and in the world. Whether it's teaching in your
large groups or discussions in your small groups, focus on the
Word of God. It's what will change men's hearts, minds and
lives. Just meeting together won't do it.

It's possible, of course, to present the truths of Scripture in
many creative ways—and in many not-so-creative ways.
Here's a principle we live by that may help: We "give them
what they need in the guise of what they want." You can give
them what they want—a seminar on parenting, for example—
to give them what they need: basic principles straight from
Scripture that teach them *more* than how to get their kids to
behave. You can show them how to motivate their kids to follow God from the heart.

These eleven principles aren't exhaustive. But they are key
principles to keep in mind as you move forward in developing
and evaluating your ministry.

Exercise 4—Looking At All the Pieces

You probably came to this book with ideas of what your
men's ministry should look like. You heard more ideas as you
surveyed your men. In the next chapter you will start to sketch
a plan for your ministry. But do some evaluation of your cur-

rent ideas as well as programs you might already have in place.

1. If ministry is a progression, does everything you do fit into that progression? Does it accomplish what you are trying to do? Is there anything you need to get rid of? What are you moving your men toward?

2. How difficult is it for men to get started in your ministry? How many easy, non-threatening entry points are there into the ministry? Where can you swing open some more doors?

3. How do you plan to grow the men from where they are when they come in? Can the men identify these step-by-step growth opportunities?

4. How well does your ministry fit the culture of your church and the men who attend the church?

5. Are you allowing ministry to happen in God's timing or are you trying to force things to happen?

6. Do your men have a wide variety of ways to serve in the church? What limits do they face?

7. Is your ministry church-based, marketplace-based or balanced?

8. What affinity groups do you see among your men that may be natural bonds for evangelism or small groups?

9. How are your men being taught to feed from the Word of God themselves? In what ways do you see them settling for scraps from others?

10. Are your men more sold on your church-based ministry or parachurch activities?

Notes

1. Karen M. Feaver, "The Soul of the Senate," *Christianity Today*, article on Richard Halverson (January 9, 1995), p. 27.
2. Archbishop William Temple, Archbishops' Committee on Enquiry on the Evangelistic Work of the Church, 1918, p. 25.
3. Bill Hybels and Mark Mittelberg (Grand Rapids, Mich.: Zondervan Publishing House, 1994).
4. Paul Little (Downers Grove, Ill.: InterVarsity Press, 1966).
5. John Stott, "The Living God Is a Missionary God," article in *Perspectives on the World Christian Movement* (Pasadena, Calif.: William Carey Library, 1981), p. 18.

Developing a
Game Plan

For NFL players, Tuesdays is playday. It's the day players usually have off—to mend wounds, fish, hunt or just hang out at home and enjoy their wife and kids. For the coaches, though, Tuesday is a workday. It's when the offensive and defensive coaches head to separate rooms and develop their plan for the upcoming game. While coaches do some of this strategic work during the summer, most of it happens on Monday and Tuesday of game week. Coaches view and review films, study the enemy's weaknesses and strengths, design schemes and develop plays—all with the purpose of using the talent at hand to its fullest.

We're at the same point in the development of your men's ministry. You have done the preliminary work. Now we're ready to get to work designing a game plan for your unique situation. I will outline in this chapter the steps you can take to write a purpose statement, develop a strategy and lay out a timeline for your ministry. You leadership types will shine. You administrative types will eat this up.

There's no getting around the fact that to do serious planning you need a place and time where you can concentrate.

This is too important to developing your ministry to hurry through the exercises. It takes time to do your planning right. It takes more time to do it wrong. Try one of the following options to make quality *and* quantity planning time happen:

Option 1: *Weekend Retreat.* You might choose to take your leadership team to a local retreat center where you can spend Friday evening through Saturday evening working through the material. You probably have plenty of retreat centers around, but scout out the following to make best use of your time:

a. *A spot close to home* so you don't spend all your time driving.

b. *Food prepared for you* so you don't spend all your time cooking and cleaning up.

c. *A quiet meeting room* where you can relax, talk, pray and work through the material.

d. *Decent sleeping facilities* so you get a good night of sleep.

e. *A flip chart* for writing down all your ideas and thoughts. You may come back to something you thought of at the start of your time together.

f. Allow for some *free time.* You won't be able to keep working at an intense level for hours on end. Plan into your weekend time to take walks, go swimming or hang out.

Option 2: *Four Evenings.* If you can't free up time for a retreat, try four consecutive Monday evenings. It gives you the same amount of work time, just spread out. One benefit of this option is that it gives you in-between think time. Make sure you still seek out a spot that is quiet and removed from any distractions—a home where the kids are gone for the evening or a room at church might work. I know of one leadership team that rented a conference room at a local hotel so they would have a sense of work while they did their planning.

Option 3: *Two All-Day Saturdays.* These are a little tougher to plan because most men make Saturdays family day. You could do one Saturday, then wait a month to meet a second

Saturday. Again you get in-between time to run your ideas past other people.

Brainstorming

You might think of other ways to structure your planning time. But no matter where or when you decide to meet there are several steps you can work through to put together your game plan. You might not find each part of the process necessary to your situation, but each is designed to help the process along.

The first step—brainstorming ministry ideas—may be the most exciting and rewarding for you as a leader. Having tabulated all the surveys and culled some general themes, you can get down to business and bring focus to the ministry. Brainstorming is how you take general ideas and begin to make them into something that begins to look like a ministry.

You can limit this activity to the small group of men on your leadership retreat, but it's even better to do it with a larger group of men *before* you go. It's a way to give men *ownership* of the ministry and *excitement* for the ministry. I built our larger brainstorming group two ways. First, once I had completed all of the individual surveys, I notified those men that we would meet in a few weeks to share the information gathered and to brainstorm further on the issues they raised. Of the sixty men interviewed, forty showed up to continue the process. What I saw was that the time I had taken to personally involve these men through the interview process had already raised their stake in the ministry. Second, I invited all the men who had indicated on the churchwide survey that they wanted to help with the men's ministry.

I began the meeting by sharing the results of the survey. I then broke the men into random small groups for brainstorming, giving them five areas to discuss for ten minutes each. These were five areas that had stood out during our survey work—we talked through, for example, how to get men into small groups, what to do once the men are plugged in, how to train leaders. Your top five concerns may be totally different from ours.

At the end of the brainstorming time, each man ranked on a 3×5 card his top three ideas from all the ones recorded. Each man then shared his rankings with the rest of the group, so that in the end each group produced three or four ideas they ranked the highest. They did this for each of the areas I wanted them to discuss. Then they came back to the large group with their three top suggestions for small groups—and what an incredible time that was. It was one of the most exciting hours of my life to hear each group stand up and share their ideas, visions, dreams and plans. We passed on all of the men's 3×5 cards of ideas and suggestions to the leadership team for tabulation—so we didn't waste any ideas. I can look back almost five years at the notes from that initial brainstorming session and see there in basic form what we are doing today.

To sum up, here are some general guidelines you should share with the guys before they break into their groups:

1. Accept and record all ideas.

2. Don't comment on anyone else's ideas during the brainstorming process.

3. Save time at the end to discuss the ideas and refine the suggestions.

4. Don't start to draw conclusions—this meeting is for generating ideas, not setting forth plans.

Here's an overview of the process we used:

1. All ideas within a group are shared and written on a chalk board or flip chart.

2. Individually the men write on a 3×5 card their top three choices out of the many suggested.

3. Each man around the circle shares his number one choice. That pick gets three points. His second choice gets two. His third choice gets one.

4. The numbers are totaled up and the top three or four ideas move on to the larger group.

Settle on a Purpose

Not everyone who took part in the brainstorming process joined our leadership team. But many did. To have so many guys involved in the brainstorming session really generates an infectious enthusiasm and excitement.

With your brainstorming complete it is time to move on to the most critical step in the whole process—defining your purpose. Pinpointing the goal of your ministry isn't something you can do in a large group—this is definitely a task for your planning retreat or meetings.

Without a clear and concise purpose it will be very difficult for your ministry to stay on track. It is very easy to plan a lot of nice and exciting meetings and activities, but not have a purpose. There are three related reasons why you need a purpose statement for your ministry:

1. *A purpose statement keeps from taking on more than you can handle.* Every time I go to a leadership planning meeting I find myself saying the same thing: "How does this fit into our purpose?" Just this noontime I met with two coordinators from our ministry. They told me all of the things they wanted next year—great ideas, but I had to pop the big purpose question. *What is our purpose for the men's ministry? And of your part of the ministry?* The discussion that followed got us back on track.

It's too easy to do activity for the sake of activity. You can always revisit your purpose statement. It can evolve over time. But having a purpose statement that is short and sweet keeps what you do fitting within the big picture.

2. *A purpose statement helps you make decisions.* When someone has a new idea for a ministry there are two questions I always ask: (a) *Who is going to lead it?* and (b) *What is its purpose?* Without a purpose statement, deciding for or against a ministry can be tough. With a purpose statement, you aren't deciding on the basis of egos, slick presentations or what happens to sound fun at the moment. Because everyone has

signed on knowing our purpose statement, it's the one fair way to determine which ideas work for us and which don't. Our coordinators meetings are much smoother when we keep in mind the overriding purpose of the ministry.

3. *A purpose statement keeps you working at your strengths.* You can do many things. But what have you decided is the *best* thing? Most ministries try to do too many things. It's better to start slow and simple. Reach one group of people and minister to them effectively before you move on to another group. A well-designed purpose statement keeps you on-task.

It would be easy to swipe someone else's statement and I have been tempted to do that many times. But the real benefit of working through your mission yourselves is *ownership*. In the end you may end up with a statement identical to what some other group has chosen. That's fine. You know that you went through the process and determined what God has put in your own hearts.

You can start the process of writing your purpose statement by having the leadership team read as many passages of scripture as possible that are relevant to your ministry's mission. You can come prepared with some, and have the group share some as well. (For example: Matthew 28:19–20; Ephesians 4:11–12; Colossians 2:6–7; Acts 1:8; John 13:34–35.) This exercise will help you focus on where you believe God is leading your ministry.

Exercise 1—God's Purpose and Your Purpose

1. Make a list of verses that have to do with God's purpose for your ministry.

2. With these in mind, pull out themes that highlight what you believe God could be calling your ministry to. You will find it helpful to write down some of the key phrases or words that come from the verses you read and study (for example: equip men, evangelize men, mobilize men for service, build disciples, engage the community, reconcile men to . . . , instruct men in . . .). Make the list as long as you can.

Exercise 2—Defining Your Purpose

1. Taking time to talk and pray, narrow your list from the second question in Exercise 1 to phrases you believe give direction to your ministry.

   (a)

   (b)

   (c)

   (d)

   (e)

   (f)

2. Write a rough draft of your purpose statement. You might want to start off your statement with something like, "Our ministry exists to glorify Jesus by . . ." Remember, what you write will tell you and others what the main business of your ministry is.

3. Refine your purpose statement. Here are some questions to ask yourselves:
   (a) Is it clear and concise—not over two sentences?

   (b) Does it state what we are about as a ministry?

   (c) Is it easy to communicate to the leaders and men of your church?

   (d) Does it empower us as leaders?

   (e) Is it consistent with who we are as a church?

4. Once you have settled on a purpose statement, take time to evaluate it. Pray over it, work on its grammar and phrasing. Share it with others and get their input. As a leadership group, come back to it in a month and see if it is still what you want. Make notes here of changes you need to make.

Down the road it will be important to have a purpose statement for each ministry you develop within the men's ministry. If you develop small groups, for example, work those leaders through the process of developing a mission statement of their own that flows from the overarching one. In the past month our Top Gun leadership team has been meeting early Friday mornings to work through the mission statement for that component of our ministry. As an outside observer it was exciting and gratifying to see these men wrestle with what their part of the ministry is to be about. With the purpose statement in hand, they have a greater sense of mission and ownership in the ministry.

You're probably curious as to what the purpose statements of other men's groups look like. This is ours:

> The purpose of the Elmbrook Men's Ministry is to encourage and equip men to evangelize the lost, establish them in their faith and equip them for service in Milwaukee, Wisconsin, and the World.

Another ministry says it this way:

> The Men's Ministry exists to make disciples who will

*build a movement of multiplying groups to bring Christ
to all of Milwaukee, Wisconsin, and beyond.*

Fond du Lac Community Church has this as their statement:

*Community Church's Men's Ministry is dedicated to
creating opportunities for men to develop vital friendships, personal integrity and profound Christ-centered
growth.*

Structuring Your Ministry

You need to know *what* you want to do. But you also need
to decide *how* you are going to do it. In this step you will determine as a leadership team how you will structure your ministry to accomplish your mission.

This isn't an easy step for most people. Our natural tendency is to do ministry the way it's always been done. Or to
grab an idea from a book or magazine or conference. But to
develop a life-changing ministry you need programs that
work best for *your* people in *your* congregation. For some of
you it may be a monthly Saturday breakfast. For others it
may be a once-a-quarter evening rally. For others a Sunday
school class just for men—and maybe only part of the year.
Every situation presents different needs. Every situation
holds different opportunities. So every situation demands a
different approach.

Now is your time to identify the best place for you to start.
As you work through the following exercise, think long-term.
Give yourself time. Start wondering what programs you can
put in place over the next *five years* to accomplish your mission statement. Don't forget to draw on all of the information
you have gathered—from interviews, surveys, meetings with
your pastor and other church leadership, and your brainstorming sessions.

Exercise 3—Structuring Our Men's Ministry

1. *Tell what you know about the men of your church and your area:*
   What are their top five needs?

   What do their friends need?

   When are they available?

   Where are they involved in the church already?

   Why do they need their own ministry—what can you provide that the rest of the church doesn't?

2. *Tell what you know about effective ministry to them:*
   Where will they likely come to a meeting?

   What types of special events are consistent with who they are?

What topics are they interested in?

How do they build relationships with other men?

How much time do they have to offer?

How structured should it be?

3. *Tell what you know about your leadership team:*
   What is your greatest strength?

   What is your greatest weakness?

   If you had to do a men's event tomorrow, what could you do well?

4. *Tell what you know about your church:*
   What types of ministries have been successful in your church? Why?

What expectations does the church leadership have for what you do?

5. Given your answers to the questions above, what elements would you like to include in your ministry to men? (evening small groups, weekly large group, monthly large group, quarterly large group, etc.)

6. Use your purpose statement to filter through these ideas. Which ideas help you reach your goals? Which ideas should you set aside because they don't directly help you to reach your goals?

7. Where should you start? What *one* program would be most effective and relatively easy to initiate within the next year?

8. What additional programs do you want to see happen over the next several years? In what order?

Timeline the Ministry

Once you have decided where to start, your next step is to plan exactly how to make it happen. To project managers out there this will sound very familiar—and even those of us who don't manage timelines day to day can use some of the great software designed to help this process. Whether you plot your ministry on-screen or on paper, what you want to do is *put things in order*, because some things can't happen until other things take place first. And you need to *break the jobs down* into manageable tasks with manageable deadlines. Developing an entire men's ministry can be utterly overwhelming, but looking at small steps along the way feels much more achievable.

When I began our men's ministry, for example, I knew I had to do two things the first year—raise the identity of the ministry and develop leadership for the ministry. I was committed to this for the long haul, and for the ministry to grow I needed solid leaders. So the first ministry we started was Top Gun, a nine-month leadership training program designed to encourage and equip men to lead in their home, workplace, church, community and world. My sole purpose was to develop a small number of leaders who would be responsible for the ministry in the future. Of the twenty-four men who went through the program the first year, eighteen hold key leadership roles for us now. Those two steps were small enough to handle, yet big enough to get us on the right path.

Three points to remember here. First, think long-term and go slow! I can't say it enough. You won't develop your ministry overnight. Even if you put in place one or two straightforward programs, what you do needs ongoing evaluation and innovation to stay fresh. When I consult with churches everyone wants a big men's ministry right away. It just doesn't happen that way. A well-rounded, full-blown ministry takes years to happen. Second, you need to choose one area to work on— leadership development, small groups, a men's retreat. It is more important to do one ministry well than to do a bunch poorly. When men sense you are doing things with excellence and purpose they will be drawn in and pull others in besides. Each year you can add one or two more components to the ministry, taking strategic steps you outline in your five-year plan. And third, what works in one church may not work in another. There is no magic formula for doing ministry. One of the scariest things about putting this material in print is that someone would think that what we do at Elmbrook has to happen everywhere.

Use the following exercise to set a timeline for the major ministries you want to see happen over the next five years and to list what needs to happen to ensure the program is established and completed.

Exercise 4—A Timeline for Ministry

1. When do we want to start the various components to the ministry?
   Year One

   Year Two

   Year Three

Year Four

Year Five

2. What has to be done in the first year for each of the major
ministries we want to start?

Ministry

Task

　When done?

Task

　When done?

Task

　When done?

Ministry

Task

　When done?

Task

　When done?

Task

　When done?

3. Step back and consider: Are the goals you have set for
each year of your ministry realistic? Measurable? Open to
evaluation? Flexible?

Divide Up Responsibilities

This is the easy part. When you have a list of everything to be done for your first ministry, assign people to do them. We'll look in detail in the next chapters at what kind of help you need to make your plans happen, but at this point you might want to work on a list of other people to help you. Go back to Question 2 in the last exercise and jot names of men who may be able to help you with each task.

Wrapping Up Your Retreat or Planning Sessions

When I coached high school football we spent Saturdays watching film from the night before and putting together our game plan for the next week. The room where we met had a sign in it that said *K.I.S.S.* When I first started I had to ask one of the other assistants what *K.I.S.S.* stood for. I should have known. *Keep It Simple, Stupid.* It was a principle we reminded ourselves of every time we drew up a game plan.

It's not a bad slogan for ministry as well. It's easy to come up with great ideas and schemes—but if your people can't execute them they aren't much use. What you have accomplished in your planning retreat or planning sessions now needs to be evaluated over the course of time by your leadership team and the men of your church. Take what you have done and let it simmer for a few months. By giving yourselves time you will be able to pray over your plans, think through them and refine them—and boil them down to what you can really do. To be honest, this is the most difficult part of the process. I know several ministries that have taken up to a year to work through all this.

So take your time. And keep it simple.

Exercise 5—Revisiting Our Plans

Give yourself at least a month after your initial planning sessions before your leadership team considers the following questions.

1. Are your plans realistic? Are there any ideas that seemed good during your initial planning that you need to reconsider?

2. What obstacles do you see to your plans? How can you overcome them?

3. Refine your decisions. What changes do you need to make to your plans?

Game Day

After hours of lifting and running, months of preparation and practice, there's nothing like Game Day. Everyone senses something big is about to crash in. The band plays, the fans cheer, the air is electric. Everybody knows this is no scrimmage. This time the score at the end of the game counts.

It's no different in ministry. You have spent months planning, praying and preparing. Now it's time to do it. You *Type A's* have surely struggled with all my planning talk. The next four chapters of this book are for you—the doers. In this final section of the book I will move through different aspects of a ministry and get practical about how a men's ministry happens. In this chapter I will outline how you can carry out special events and monthly meetings. In the following two chapters I will discuss small groups and leadership development, and in the final chapter I will talk about "Special Teams" play—short-term missions and evangelism among men.

Special Events

I am starting with special events because they are the easiest way to get a men's ministry going. Besides that, you can

stretch and reshape almost anything you do—a retreat, barbecue, sports outing, rally night or something else—to serve a
specific purpose within your ministry. If you remember my
diagram from Chapter 5, special events are on the bottom of
my funnel illustration. So what do they accomplish?

Special events raise the identity of your ministry. If you are
just starting your ministry, special large group gatherings let
men of your church hear about the ministry and its plans. I
use these events to paint with broad stokes our vision of the
ministry, or to detail some new program we will start in the
near future. Some churches decide to do two major events for
their men during the first year of their men's ministry, using
these events to spark the men's interest and to convey to them
plans for the upcoming year.

*Special events can be a safe place for a new man to come
or to bring another man.* You can plan most special events as
entry points into your ministry. They can be a place where a
man is encouraged to simply come and listen—and not feel
compelled to speak his opinions, share his feelings or discuss
his deepest sins. Rather, he can receive ministry and have an
opportunity to fellowship with other men from the church.

*Special events are a chance for men to be gently encour-
aged to go deeper.* We do special events fully knowing new
men will attend. So we often have a testimony from someone
who has participated in a small group. At the conclusion of
the event we give men the chance to take the next step beyond
our large, relatively anonymous events and join a small group.
Most of the small groups we have going right now grew out of
special events.

Special events develop leaders. Many of the key leaders in
our ministry are men who started on one of our special event
committees. Activities pull men into service. As leaders we
spend considerable time thinking of all the things that need
to get done for an event to really cook—and then think of all
the men we can draw in. Because these events have a defined
start and finish and because men love activity we usually find

many men who are open to getting involved.

Special events give men time with other men. Special events let men just hang out. Often the different parts of our ministry become segregated, with some men active in one part and other men active in another. At a special event all the men come together and hear what is going on with men they normally don't see or talk to.

Special events are a great way to kick off a new year. Special events give your leadership team a platform to explain what the upcoming year looks like and sign men up for the activities. At our fall special events we set up publicity tables for each of the various parts of our ministry in order to make them all visible. Then the men stop by what interests them and we enlist men for the year. Many ministries find it helpful to have a fall men's retreat. It brings men together, gives them a taste of small groups and lets the leadership share their vision with the men.

I hope it is obvious by now that I love special events and strongly believe they do a men's ministry a lot of good. We used them in a big way the first couple of years to get our ministry going. Just doing events lets men know the ministry is up and running.

Events are safe. They don't require men to go deep. Unfortunately, some men equate activities with ministry. Some men's ministries are being planned and orchestrated so guys can jump from one activity to another without ever going further than showing up. Special events are vital to a well-rounded men's ministry. But you can't base your entire ministry on them! It's tempting to overdo them. They're great to build numbers. But if you don't move your men into individual ministries you will do them a gigantic disservice.

In Appendix B of this book I have compiled a list of fifteen potential special events—from breakfasts to golf events to trips and retreats—with a word or two on what to keep in mind for each. For the rest of this chapter we will look at strategies that make all special events work.

Your Special Events Planning Team

To pull off an event without burning out yourself or another leadership member, you want to build a team of men to work together. You will not only spare your sanity, you will give other men a chance to grow in leadership.

I won't start without a coordinator, or better yet, *co*-coordinators. We have found the idea of *co*-coordinators works well in spreading around responsibility and building accountability. With my help these co-coordinators recruit the rest of the team members. It's important when they recruit men for the team that they detail what each man will be doing. Men want to know what tasks they're getting themselves into—and how long the job will take. They won't offer to help next time if you pop too many surprises on them.

For the sake of discussion, I will look at how you could pull together what you need for a fall ministry kickoff to happen on a Friday evening. The purpose of the get-together is to inform the men of your church about what will be happening in the men's ministry in the coming year and give them a chance to come together to worship, fellowship and receive some general teaching on what it means to be a godly man. The event will happen at church on a Friday evening in early September.

The following is a list of the team members you will want for a kickoff and their job descriptions. This may look rather intimidating—possibly nine guys to recruit. There are at least five reasons to work hard, though, to recruit as many men as you can to help. Getting more help:

1. Spreads out responsibility and cuts down on burnout
2. Gives more men in the church ownership of the ministry

3. Fosters a team spirit
4. Develops more leadership for the ministry
5. Provides more resources for ideas and contacts.

Keep in mind, though, that depending on the size of your group and the type of event you plan, some men might be able to handle two of the areas. Maybe those nine guys are the only nine men you expect to attend. Then consider this your special event to-do list.

Chairperson

1. Recruits committee members with the help of the men's ministry leadership team.
2. Organizes committee meetings.
3. Keeps the leadership team up to date.
4. Serves as a resource for committee members.
5. Develops the timetable for things to be accomplished.
6. Prays for the committee members.
7. Coordinates the evaluation process.
8. Encourages the committee members in their tasks.
9. Makes sure the committee members get things done on time.

Publicity Coordinator

1. Designs, writes and reproduces brochure or flyer (see end of chapter for some ideas).
2. Mails brochure to individuals in the church, with cover letter from leadership team—may include yearly brochure as well.
3. Makes posters for event and has them placed around the church one month before event.
4. Talks to pastor about having an announcement from the pulpit a few weeks before event.

Budget Manager

1. Sets deadline for budget requests.
2. Helps chairman set price for the event—including money

for food, publicity, honorariums, materials, facility use, and rentals or transportation, if needed. It's best to set a budget that covers your event costs even if you have a modest turnout. Any extra goes toward next year's event.

3. Networks with registration coordinator to get money into proper account.
4. Ensures all bills are paid.
5. Provides change and collects proceeds from on-site registration at the event.

Registration Coordinator

1. Recruits team of volunteers to sell tickets on Sunday mornings and handle mail-in registrations.
2. Enters registrations into computer (you want to keep track of who comes to help you plan future events—as well as to form a list of potential helpers).
3. Coordinates pre-paid and walk-in registrations on the day of the event.
4. Recruits team to register people at event.
5. Coordinates with budget person to get money into proper account.

Facilities Coordinator

1. Recruits team of volunteers.
2. Reserves rooms for event—prayer room, fellowship hall, kitchen, chapel.
3. Recruits team to help move equipment on and off stage, as needed.
4. Coordinates with Christian bookstore if you want books sold at the event.
5. Coordinates with church facilities person for setup (chairs, registration tables, publicity tables, etc.).

Hospitality Coordinator

1. Recruits ushers for the event and trains them.
2. Recruits greeters for the event.
3. Recruits team to serve refreshments after the event.

Program Coordinator

1. Recruits team to handle the event's logistics.
2. Plans the program with the help of chairperson.
3. Works with technical people on slide shows, lighting, sound.
4. Contacts the people involved (worship team, special music, testimonies, speakers, emcee, prayer people) to make sure they know what is happening.

Food Guy—(Don't forget the food guy!)

1. Recruits men to help prepare the food.
2. Puts the menu together and orders the food.
3. Gets everything together necessary to cook.
4. Oversees preparation and serving of food on the night of the event.
5. Cleans up the facilities when finished or sees that it gets done.

Prayer Coordinator

1. Obtains prayer requests from the various coordinators on a monthly basis.
2. Distributes prayer requests to prayer teams from the church.
3. Mobilizes a team of men to pray during the event.

Death by Committee

The last thing you want is for your committee meetings to mimic the boring meetings most men endure at work. Once you have recruited your working committee your first step is to call a planning meeting. At that meeting you have two major tasks: team building and decision making. Spend the first hour of your meeting getting to know one another through team building and discussion exercises. (Have a barbecue. Break the committee into groups of three after sharing and prayer for the first thirty minutes. Spend the first meeting with every man sharing how he became a Christian and why he wants to be on the committee. Or have the men share their most embarrassing moment.) Then spend time in prayer for the event—*before* you make your decisions. Some of the major decisions you need to work through in your first few meetings:

What is the purpose of the event? You must decide early on this one. Don't just *do* an event—know *why* you're doing it. Is it an evangelistic outreach, instruction for believers, a time of fellowship, worship or something else? Should it cover a specific issue like finances or parenting or is it going to be more general?

Who is it for? Is it for the men of our church only or for the community at large?

When is it going to be? Friday evening, Saturday morning, Sunday evening, during the week? What is the best time for the men of your church?

Where should we have it? At the church, at a retreat center, at a local banquet hall? This will be tied in to the purpose of the event. If it is an evangelistic breakfast, for example, you might want to move it out of the church and onto men's turf— such as a banquet room of a local hotel.

What will you include in the program? Speaker, testimonies, slide show of past events, drama, small-group discussion, prayer time, worship time and vision sharing are just a few options.

Will you serve food? Is it going to be a burger roast or coffee and rolls, catered or you-cook-it, or just refreshments?

Committee Meetings

For a large event your working committee probably needs to meet monthly. Learn to run these meetings allowing for on-task planning and for God's spontaneity. Start on time and let the men go at a time you have agreed on beforehand. Evening meetings that are done in two hours might follow this format:

7:00–7:10 Catching up
7:10–7:20 Devotions

7:20–8:15   Committee Reports (program, budget, facilities, publicity, hospitality, etc.). Each committee member takes time to bring other members up to speed on what he has been doing in his area as well as to get input on any decisions he needs to make.

8:15–8:30   Prayer for event and other issues raised during the reports.

8:30–9:00   New Business

A Special Event Timeline

Once you have decided what you want to do and when you will do it, put together a timeline for all the things you need to complete. You may be able to stage events in much less time than we do. If you know you can do it, adjust this timetable to your own schedule. You can't get around doing some points—like facility reservations—far in advance. But consider this as a model of how to give yourself enough time to not push anyone over the edge:

Nine Months Ahead
   Co-coordinators recruited for the event
   Committee pulled together by the co-coordinators

Seven Months Ahead
   First committee meeting
   Team members get to know one another and pray together
   Decisions made on what the event will look like
   Dates set for future monthly meetings
   Letters sent out to speakers
   Rooms at church reserved (gym, kitchen, fellowship hall and chapel)

Six Months Ahead
   List of committee members distributed
   Timeline put together and job descriptions finalized
   Committee members recruit men to serve with them in their areas

Committee members secure prices for their specific area
(the food people, for example, determine how much it
will cost per man for the dinner portion—hamburgers,
salads, chips, soda, buns, etc.)

Five Months Ahead

Budget developed for the event and price determined
All of the participants for the event are contacted and se-
cured (for example: worship leaders, men to give tes-
timonies, drama team and emcee for the evening)
Work begun on the brochure or flyer for the event
Accommodations reserved for guests

Four Months Ahead

Rough draft of brochure examined and changes made
Date of event is included in men's ministry mailings
Leaders recruited for follow-up small groups

Three Months Ahead

Brochures and posters printed
Sound people contacted and given preliminary outline for
evening

Two Months Ahead

Mailing sent to all men of the church and to any other local
churches involved
Final program defined and timed out (see example)
Music selected, overheads made and copyrights obtained
if not already done so
Slide show assembled
Posters put up around church
Registration table staffed on Sunday mornings to take reg-
istrations and handle questions about the event
Training for small group leaders takes place
Bulletin announcements placed with church office
Men assigned to care for any special guest (seminar speak-
ers, keynote speakers, musicians, etc.)

One Month Ahead

Material printed for evening
Program for the evening finalized

Name tags bought
Evaluation forms prepared and printed
Small group sign-up sheets prepared
All speakers contacted for any special requests
Food ordered
Room setups coordinated with church custodial staff
Date set for evaluation meeting by working committee
Week of Event
Final headcount sent to those cooking
Signs made to direct men around church (if needed)
Honorarium checks cut for the guests speakers, etc.

The Big Day

It's easy to forget details on the big day. Use this sample schedule for starters:

12:00 M. — Setup begins
Gym: tables setup with chairs, decorations
Registration tables set up
Grills set up
Sanctuary set up: screens, worship band, sound system
Ministry tables set up

5:30 P.M. — Begin to serve food in the gym
6:30 P.M. — Concert in the sanctuary
7:00 P.M. — Program begins
Slide show (2 minutes)
Welcome by the emcee
Overview of the evening (5 minutes)
Crowd breaker (10 minutes)
Worship: Men's Worship Band (10 minutes)
Overview of upcoming ministry (10 minutes)
Testimony by man influenced by
    men's ministry (3 minutes)
Worship (10 minutes)
Drama (5 minutes)
Speaker (35 minutes)

Wrap-up: thank people and speaker, remind about refreshments afterward
8:30 P.M. — Reception in Fellowship Hall
9:30 P.M. — Cleanup

Keys to a Successful Special Event

Good special events don't just happen. Here's what holds
them together:

1. *Specific purpose.* Early on in the planning process you
agree on the purpose of the event so you aren't all trying to do
different things. Every event you do cannot meet all the needs
of the men. Be specific.

2. *Give away responsibility.* While one or two men could
probably do an event by themselves it isn't beneficial to them
or the men of the church. Special events are opportunities to
get others involved and give them a chance to serve.

3. *Timing.* Make sure you plan your event with the whole
church calendar in mind. It's easy to play maverick in the ministry, but you're a part of the church. Make sure you don't
hinder other ministries by the timing of your event. Case in
point: Don't plan a men's retreat the weekend after a couple's
retreat, or plan a men's event on Valentine's Day or Mother's
Day—yep, it's been done.

4. *Evaluate.* If an event is worth doing it is worth evaluating for the next time. Give the men time at the event to evaluate what they thought of the event and to make suggestions
for the future. After the event, hold an evaluation meeting
when you can go over the evaluations and plan for the future.

Evaluations work best when done both by participants and
by the men who organized and carried out the program. After
an evangelistic outreach luncheon with Frank Tanna, former
Detroit Tigers pitcher, I sent a letter to ten men who attended
the luncheon and brought a friend. I asked questions like the
following:

1. Was the setting where we met appropriate for what we were trying to do?   Yes ☐   No ☐

2. Was the service at your table
            Poor ☐   Average ☐   Excellent ☐

3. Was the food hot when it reached your table?
                                Yes ☐   No ☐

4. Was the message clear?   Yes ☐   No ☐

5. Did the program allow for follow-up of the discussion on the way back to work?   Yes ☐   No ☐

6. What should we change the next time we do an event like this one?

7. What should we do the same?

8. What recommendations do you have for the planning committee?

With these evaluations in hand, the working committee does its own evaluation. We plan an evaluation meeting for a week or so after the event, while everything is still fresh in everyone's mind. Go through each aspect of the event and ask the tough questions—regarding publicity: Was the flyer/brochure out in time? Was the brochure clear to both those who invited others and to those who were being invited? Did we use every means possible to get men to the event? What could we do differently next time?

This can be a grueling, even painful process. But it will help your men learn and prepare for next time—even if next time is a completely different program or event. What kind of evaluations you do will depend on what kind of event you did. Some need only a quick ten-minute meeting after the event. Others need a full evening of discussion.

Monthly Large Group Meetings

In the same way special events held a couple of times a year have an important role to play, so do monthly meetings. In the grand scheme of things these involve a little more commitment by the leaders—and a little more involvement on the part of the men. There are a lot of reasons for having a regular scheduled meeting. It

provides an opportunity for your church's men to gather regularly for fellowship.

creates a place for new men in the church to get involved in the men's ministry with a modest time commitment, in a non-threatening environment.

builds a springboard for men to get involved in small groups.

serves as the hub for all your men's ministry activities. With men involved in various small groups, committees and ministries, this is their chance to come together and share what God is doing in their lives and in their ministries.

establishes a place where the vision of the ministry can constantly be shared and upcoming events discussed.

provides a place for leadership to develop. You can train future small group leaders by having them lead discussion groups at the meeting.

Here's what you need to begin a monthly large group ministry:

1. *Develop a leadership team.* You will want *co-coordinators*—they call the meetings, develop the team, make sure every man on the committee is doing his job. *Publicity*—to

place bulletin announcements, to inform the church newsletter, to send reminders. *Cooking*—to prepare the meal or refreshments for each meeting. *Program*—to line up speakers, music, testimonies, emcee, multimedia. *Table talk*—to recruit discussion leaders, make sure the speaker has questions for discussions that are tied in to his talk. *Greeters*—to meet the men when they arrive and give them name tags. This committee can meet right after the meeting to evaluate and go over any details for the next meeting.

2. *Develop a purpose statement.* Don't shoot me—but here I go again. Your team needs to develop a purpose statement. Our men wrote this: "The Saturday Breakfast Fellowship exists to provide an opportunity for the Men of Elmbrook to have fellowship and find encouragement on a monthly basis." Allow your team time to think through and discuss why they want to meet and how it fits into the big scheme of things for the men's ministry.

3. *Decide on a structure.* There are a lot of ways to do what you want to do. Everything depends on your specific church situation and when your men prefer to meet. Below are two formats very different from each other—but each work well in various churches:

Monthly Saturday Breakfast
7:30–8:00	Eat breakfast
8:00–8:10	Announcements
8:10–8:30	Worship
8:30–9:00	Speaker
9:00–9:30	Table discussion

Monthly Wednesday Evening
6:30–7:00	Worship and announcements
7:00–7:35	Speaker
7:35–8:15	Refreshments

4. *Line up speakers.* There is no magical way to do this.

Wherever you find your speakers, schedule them as far in advance as possible. Some churches I work with use outside speakers exclusively. By using leaders from sports, business and the church at large they let their men and their guests hear from a wide variety of men. Other places—like Elmbrook—use just one person to provide a series for the year. In my case our meetings are the one opportunity I have to address the men on a monthly basis. The consistency is helpful. You might want to ask your pastor if he would like to speak at these monthly events. If you use outside speakers, make sure to provide an honorarium and travel expenses. If he has to stay overnight, be sure to provide lodging for him. Whether he stays at a hotel or at someone's home, give him time for rest and preparation.

5. *Develop a theme for the year.* By picking a theme for the year you tell your men you are serious about these meetings and have thought out what you want to accomplish. This year we have been working on the theme of "Running Like a Champion." All of my talks as well as the testimonies and everything else we do at those meetings have focused on that one theme.

6. *Use your meetings as a bridge.* If you remember from a couple of chapters back, one of the keys to men's ministry is moving men along in their commitment to Christ. Include things in the meetings that provide the men an opportunity to take the next step. You can announce new small group start-ups, for example, so men can join. Or you can announce a service opportunity at church. I continually ask myself this question about all we do: *How can I use this to move men forward?*

7. *Follow-up on newcomers.* One of the old principles for evangelism is to go where the Spirit leads. If a man comes to your meeting for the first time, he showed up for a reason. Maybe he wants fellowship, or encouragement or guidance. Have your leadership team call these new people and ask them how they liked it. Ask what they would change—that makes them the expert—and what they got out of it. This personal follow-up is a means to help the men feel cared for and

counted on. It may blow open doors to really minister to a man. It isn't uncommon for the guys on our team to end up in profound conversations as they make these calls.

8. *Plan your meetings carefully.* When you put together your meetings you will want to keep in mind the following:

Are there smooth transitions from one part of the meeting to the next? Does the meeting flow—or is it awkward and choppy?

Are there breaks in the meeting so the men can stretch?

Is there a chance for the men to just talk with other men? It is possible to overly structure the meeting so the men can never meet this simple need.

Do the components of the meeting fit together?

If you do music—are the overheads or songsheets easy to read? New people will feel out of place if you sing songs without printed words.

Are the seats comfortable for the men to sit on for an extended time? The heart only hears what the seat can stand.

Is a sound system necessary for the room you are using? Does it work properly? Don't use a sound system that would make an angel blaring from heaven sound like a squawking duck.

Is the message practical and relevant—meeting the men of your church where they are? Does it have points for the men to apply? Is it biblically based?

There are a wide variety of ways to do a large group meeting. These are a marvelous opportunity to minister to the men of your church, limitless in the things you can do. Large group meetings may be all you choose to do in the first year of your ministry. You can also choose to use other methods in your first years and add a large group meeting later, as we did.

Advertising Your Ministry

One thing you don't want men to say about your ministry is "I didn't even know you existed." In some congregations the men's ministry is the best kept secret in the church. Once you have worked at framing a basic program for the men, you want to press hard to raise the identity of the ministry and ensure that everyone knows what will soon take place. And when you do something, make sure you do it with excellence. It's better to do fewer things and do them right than to do a lot of things shabbily. If a man comes to a well-orchestrated event he will tell his friends—and before you know it you have a movement. Let me wrap up this chapter with some ways you can get the word out about your ministry:

A ministry brochure. You can do a brochure in a variety of styles, but create one piece that can be mailed to all of the men in the fall as well as made available to newcomers and visitors to your church.

Bulletin spots. Make someone in your ministry responsible for getting events into the bulletin at least three weeks ahead of time.

Direct mailing. Two or three times a year I send a cover letter and brochure for an upcoming event to every man in the church to inform them of what is coming up. In August I give them the Golf Outing brochure, a Top Gun (leadership training) brochure, and a general ministry brochure. In January they hear about our statewide rally, and in April or May I tell them about major summer activities.

Reminder cards. Send postcards to smaller groups of men to remind them of upcoming events. We send everyone who has attended one of our Saturday Breakfast Fellowships a card one week ahead of time to remind them of the next one.

Women's ministry. If you want the men to come to an event, go through their wives. We work hard at getting the women on our team. We are fortunate to have a thriving women's ministry in our church, and they allow me or one of my leaders to regularly announce upcoming events and pass out registration forms. I know the wives go home and tell their husbands.

Newsletter. Any sort of a regular bulletin you can do is a wonderful tool to share what has happened and what will happen in the ministry. The downside is that newsletters are a ton of work. We are in our fourth year of ministry and we still don't have one. We're looking for someone to head it up now. The advice I have received from many people is don't try to do too many issues per year. If your church has a newsletter, make sure you use it as much as possible.

Testimonies. Ask your pastor if you could periodically have someone from your ministry share on a Sunday morning what God is doing in his life as a result of your men's ministry. If you send a group of men to a Promise Keepers Conference in the summer, for example, check to see if you can have a couple of guys share when they get back.

Bulletin board/kiosk. Ask your pastor if there is a bulletin board somewhere in the church that your ministry could share or even have full-time. Work with someone to keep it up to date with upcoming events and activities.

Flyers. Make up flyers not just for the men already in your ministry but to insert in the bulletin or pass out as people leave after a Sunday service.

Word of mouth. The best of all. As men see their lives changing they will talk up your ministry.

There are bigger, splashier ways to get the word out—media, drama, music. But these are some straightforward ideas. I have to admit that I have come to appreciate the need for publicity to enable a ministry to happen. Don't be afraid to spend energy and money on marketing, if I can call it that. The money you use to get men to your activities puts them in a position to be changed through your ministry—and that is what it is all about.

Special events and monthly meetings are only a small part of what can happen in your ministry. With that base laid, let's move on to look at small groups—the places where men can meet to be encouraged, confronted, comforted, held accountable and fan the flames of faith.

Huddles: Starting Small Groups for Your Men

For the last twenty years I have been involved in countless groups in church and parachurch settings—task groups, study groups, work groups, prayer groups, evangelistic groups. One group, however, stands out. I mentioned earlier in the book that six years ago I asked two friends if they would like to meet regularly to share what was going on in our lives and to pray for one another. Never did I imagine how we would grow together. As we began to meet for an hour a week or every other week some things started to happen:

Our group became a place where I could be encouraged. Hebrews 10:24–25 tells us that believers aren't to neglect meeting together—and that when we do meet one key purpose for being together is encouragement. That's a big piece of what I gained. When one of us took a step of faith or said no to sin, the other two cheered. We covenanted to never let the others walk through the valley of death by themselves. Shortly after we started getting together I found myself in the hospital with a blown-out knee. Hardly life-threatening. But within an hour both men were there.

Our group provided a place for accountability. Men are

icebergs. People only see a tenth or so of our lives—almost always the beautiful part. What's below the surface, however, is where our real lives happen—lives often hidden from the scrutiny of other Christians. The jagged subsurface edges of my secret life often ripped open relationships and damaged my spiritual life. When my friends probed my hidden side they offered an accountability that exposed those jagged areas of my life and allowed me to be healed.

The group fanned the flames of faith. Proverbs 27:17 says that "as iron sharpens iron so one man sharpens another." Our small group was a place to talk about ways to improve my prayer life and my devotion to Christ. It helped me discover whether I was serving in the right area and if my gifts were being used.

Through the last six years I have changed ministry focus and faced personal challenges. It has been the small group that has helped hold me together. I will never *not* be in a small group, and any ministry I oversee will have a small group ministry at its core.

In this chapter I want to discuss how your leadership team can start small groups for the men of your church. To be honest, this may be the most important thing you as a leadership team can provide for your men. It's the stuff that makes disciples. There are a number of great books on how to start and run small groups, and I will mention some of them at the end of this chapter. What I will cover in this chapter won't give you every detail those books can provide regarding running a full-blown small group ministry. But let me outline some points that will get you started.

Why Men's Small Groups?

While there are many reasons why small groups will benefit your ministry to men, let me mention just a few.

Small groups allow men to share life. In 1 Thessalonians 2:8–9 Paul tells the Thessalonians he came not only to share the Gospel of Jesus Christ, but also to share his life with them. This principle is exemplified not only in the life of Paul but in the life of Jesus. This life-sharing is rare today. Our society is information hungry. We keep a distance from one another through e-mail and answering machines. Small groups break through these superficial, shallow relationships. Men can share what is really going on in their lives.

Who can a man talk to about the troubles he is having with his teenage daughter?

Who can he talk to about the emotional connectedness he feels for a gal at the office?

Who can he talk to about the wounds of his past?

Where can he go to share the joys of leading a co-worker to Christ?

Where can he share his deepest fears as a man?

The answer to all these is *the small group*. It is the biblical means by which men can get together with other men and share life with one another.

Small groups are a place to function as real Christians. A man recently walked up to me and said, "Where do I start?"

I responded by saying, "Start what?"

"Start doing everything the Bible tells me I am supposed to be doing," he said. "I go to a church with three thousand people in the service. I go to the Men's Monthly Breakfast and there are over two hundred men there—but where can I practically love, forgive, accept, and encourage another man?" Great question. There's a great answer as well: a small group. Within the New Testament there are close to one hundred and twenty "One Another Injunctions," such as:

Accept one another (Romans 15:7)

Love one another (John 13:34–35)

Encourage one another (1 Thessalonians 5:11)

Build each other up (1 Thessalonians 5:11)

Carry each other's burdens (Galatians 6:2)

Confess your sins to each other (James 5:16)

Pray for each other (James 5:16)

Instruct one another (Romans 15:14)

Each of these commands can be lived out in a small group. In a group of four to twelve men you can love another, pray for another, carry another's burden, accept others the way they are, and forgive others when wronged. Given our frantic lives, those things are hard to do outside a small group!

Small groups grow men in Christ. In Colossians 1:28 Paul says his goal of teaching is to present every man "perfect in Christ." Not a bad goal for a men's ministry. Within the confines of a small group men can learn what Christianity is all about. By working through a curriculum like *Operation Timothy*, they will be grounded. Or by studying Romans they will learn the great doctrines of our faith. Not only do they discuss what God desires, men get a chance to apply what they learn— and to be held accountable for areas they want to change. The bottom line is that in small groups men become more and more like Christ in all they say and do. If the group ever loses this component they are finished. Bill Hybels, senior pastor at Willow Creek Community Church in Chicago, says, "No Christian will ever actualize his or her spiritual potential unless they are in a small group. The highest goal of any small group is to grow in Christ."[1]

Small groups offer accountability. One of the failings of much of contemporary Christianity is its emphasis on individualism. Thousands upon thousands of people believe they can make a decision to become a Christian bathed in the glow of their television or amid the crush of a large gathering of people and then never face accountability for their actions the rest of their lives. Christianity for them is a solo sport. God didn't design Christianity that way. In the same way that it would be suicidal for a quarterback to play offense by himself against eleven defensive players, so it is spiritual suicide to try to live the Christian life without others. Unfortunately, many try— especially men.

In a famous survey of fallen leaders a few years ago,

Howard Hendricks, professor at Dallas Theological Seminary, interviewed either over the phone or face-to-face some 242 Christian leaders recently forced to leave the ministry because of moral failure. One of the questions he asked was if they were in an accountability group. To everyone's surprise, not a single one was. These were good men. Godly men. Leaders who desired nothing but God's best for them. Yet they fell.[2]

A small group provides the context where tough questions can be asked week in and week out. Chuck Swindoll has seven questions that give you a taste of what these questions might be like:[3]

1. Have I been with a woman in the past week in a way that could be viewed as compromising?
2. Have all my financial dealings been filled with integrity?
3. Have I viewed or read sexually explicit material?
4. Have I achieved the goals I set for Bible study and prayer?
5. Have I spent quantity time with—and given priority to—my family?
6. Have I fulfilled the mandates of my calling?
7. Have I just lied to you?

These probing questions get right to the point. They rip to the heart of men's struggles. At the end of the chapter I will include a more lengthy list that your groups can use for accountability.

Small groups maintain the momentum of a large event. Men's ministries face few challenges bigger than shepherding men who attend a Promise Keepers Conference or Wake-Up Call and come home all excited about their life in Christ. Just like high school kids returning home from a retreat, they will lose their fire unless they are put in a position to keep the flames going. If we truly want to bring the fire home to our churches and keep that fire burning, then small groups are the means. One weekend a year doesn't make a man of God. Promise Keepers is rightly putting enormous amounts of energy and time into helping men see why they need small groups. We can be there to provide small groups for the men the other fifty-one weeks of the year.

Exercise 1—Why Do Small Groups?

As a leadership team, make a list of the reasons for men to be in small groups.

1.

2.

3.

4.

5.

6.

7.

8.

Types of Small Groups

So what are our options? is what you are probably asking right about now. In this section let's look at seven types of small groups you could have within your ministry. In no way am I saying you need all of these or that these are your only options. Rather, I want to give you the big picture so you can select and start what is best for your ministry.

Task Groups

Task groups come together to work on a project. They are action-oriented, aiming at accomplishing a specific task—a great way to get men involved.

Three years ago, with one of our church's missionaries, I took three businessmen to Succeava, Romania. We wanted to help a small church get firmly rooted in that city. Our men met with a small group of Christians from the church to talk about economic development—how we could help them start a business to provide enough money to pay the pastor's salary and to run the church. Everyone decided to start a used clothing store.

To start a used clothing store, of course, you need clothes. So these guys came back and have been collecting good quality clothes from people in the church and community. To this date they have sent to Romania six forty-foot cargo containers of clothes. Some have traveled back to do business workshops. In order to keep the project going, we meet once a month in my office as a small group. We don't spend time in study, accountability or extended times of sharing, but we have become a tight bunch and seen God do a marvelous work in our midst. Although our group has a practical bent, these men are practicing the "one anothers." They definitely pass the "I-can-call-them-anytime-of-day-or-night" test. When we meet we talk about the project and what needs to happen to keep it moving forward. Our group has a specific purpose and these men love being a part of it.

Entry-Level Group

Most men cringe when they hear the word "small group." They would sooner go shopping for a day than be in a small group. It's necessary, therefore, to give men small groups in small doses. I have found that almost any man who gets into a small group grows to love it and will rarely want to leave it.

We use special events to start these groups. I have found it helpful to have groups short in length and high on application. After we had Steve Farrar do a weekend with our guys, for example, we started up eight new small groups. During the event men gave testimony about the importance of small groups and then we gave men a chance to sign up at the end of the event. The groups were formed to go through Farrar's book *Point Man* and were intended to last six weeks, meeting for an hour a week. The time was split between sharing with one another, praying for one another and discussing the material. The guys loved it. A number of those groups are still going today. Give 'em a taste and you've got 'em.

Investigative Bible Studies

Jesus made profound claims about himself that few non-Christians grasp. Investigative Bible studies pull together a number of men seeking to understand these claims. One man I know has spent considerable time building bridges with the men in his office. After a number of spiritual discussions with them, he asked them if they would be interested in joining him for a three-week study of Jesus Christ. The first week they looked at "Who Jesus Is," the second week at "What Jesus Did" and the final week at "What Is Man's Response?" These types of groups afford seekers the chance to ask questions they may not normally ask. It allows them to look at the core issues of Christianity and knocks down false caricatures of Christianity. It is exciting to hear how men have turned to Jesus as a result of this type of small group.

Accountability Groups

The purpose of accountability groups is straightforward—to come together for a short period of time to ask the tough questions, share and pray for one another. When I meet with my guys it's usually for just one hour. We each take fifteen minutes to share what is going on in our lives, tell the men what we want to be accountable for in the coming week or weeks and then spend the final fifteen minutes praying for one another. We don't study anything, work on anything or try to save anyone. This group is purely to sharpen our character and to encourage our souls. Of all the groups mentioned these are probably the easiest to get going. They can also pay some of the greatest dividends because men seldom find accountability elsewhere in the church.

Study Groups

George meets with eight men every Wednesday morning at a local restaurant. Their table is reserved and the waitress knows them by name because they've been eating in the same booth for the last six years. These guys are committed to one another and to the Word. They spend the first thirty minutes sharing with one another and eating breakfast. Then they break open the real Bread and away they go. They have worked through Genesis, Revelation, Romans and a host of other books and topics. Surely they have built relationships, but their stated purpose for meeting is to "study the Word." Unfortunately, many men in our society spend a great deal of time *under* the Word of God getting teaching, but not *in* the Word of God digging and living. It's easy to discuss what others say about the Bible and not study it for yourself. Bible study groups allow men to systematically work through various books of the Bible and to allow God to change their hearts and lives.

Support Groups

Support groups provide support and encouragement to men who are all dealing with the same life issue. For many men, these groups are the key to coping with life and getting on their feet again. The groups reach and minister to specific pockets of men with common needs. Some churches have sponsored groups for those with sexual addictions, those living with an unbelieving wife, groups based on Alcoholics Anonymous, others dealing with drug addictions and single parenthood. One somewhat unusual group I know well of is our CPR group—"Career Path Restoration." Each Monday evening Doug leads a group of men who are presently unemployed or know they will soon lose their job. While there are many groups in our area that provide practical assistance through networking, interview training and résumé help, few walk with someone through the pain of job loss. Doug and his team provide just that. They offer the loving care men need. They help group members walk through the process and enable them to see Jesus walking with them.

Top Gun Groups

Top Gun is our nine-month "men equipping men" program designed to model, teach and encourage practical application of the biblical principles that build a foundation for living life in Christ. A Top Gun group is twelve men who meet for two hours a week. They spend the first hour in small groups sharing, praying and being accountable to one another, and the second hour in the large group discussing the work they did over the course of the week. The modules include "Intimacy With Christ," "How to Study the Bible," "The Man and His Family," "Servant Leadership," "Evangelism," and "Biblical Principles for Work." Each man spends an average of two hours a week in Bible study, Bible memory and outside reading. The manual has been written by the men of our ministry and is now being used by churches all over the country. Of all the things going on in our ministry, this is by far the most exciting. It's having the biggest impact in the lives of our men. There is information on Top Gun groups in Appendix C.

Friendship Groups

Every Friday morning Paul hosts a group of about ten men in his home. Generally half are from the suburbs and half are from the city. They come from all different denominations, races and backgrounds. Some are in full-time ministry, others are not. They spend time sharing with one another, fellowshiping and praying for one another, meeting to break down the walls that exist in our city. There is no agenda, no planning or study—just men getting to know men and developing friendships. What an incredible thing to see these groups popping up all over the landscape.

Is this an exhaustive list? No. But it does cover a number of the choices for you. Small groups don't have to all be one flavor. As a leadership team you can decide which you want to use or what combination to use. If small groups are anything they are flexible—you can tailor them to your church and your men.

Recruiting and Training Small Group Leaders

When you start a small group you entrust the lives of men to a leader. That being true, you want to ensure your leaders are qualified and trained to lead. You don't recruit these men by "casting wide the net" but by "tapping men on the shoulder." Don't use the bulletin or ask for volunteers at large gatherings of men. Your leadership team or pastor or other church leaders will be the best source of names of potential leaders.

Be careful in selecting men to lead your groups. It's far more dangerous to put men in charge who aren't qualified than to not have small groups. Some qualities to look for in a leader:

1. *Godly character.* He takes knowing and loving God very seriously (1 Timothy 3:1–13).
2. *An authentic relationship with Jesus.* His relationship is characterized by obedience and submission to Christ (1 John 2:3–11).
3. *A consistent walk in the power of the Holy Spirit.* He daily yields to His work in his life (Ephesians 5:18–21).
4. *Spiritual giftedness.* He shows gifts in the area of leading a discussion and engaging others (1 Corinthians 12:7ff.).

5. *A teachable spirit.* He is open to learn from others and God.
6. *A commitment to building and multiplying disciples to reach the world.* He has a vision for the harvest and for building disciples to go into the harvest (Matthew 28:19–20).
7. *Has been in a group already.* Having been a participant gives him the practical experience he needs to lead others.

After praying over your list of potential leaders and sensing these men are ready to lead, you can then approach them with the job description. Spell out clearly what you expect, the job they would do and how long they will need to be involved. Some expectations to include are:

He attends church regularly.
He makes devotions a priority.
He will attend all the training sessions.
He can make a one-year commitment.
He will come fully prepared to each meeting.
He will develop a prayer team for himself as he leads the group.

With the leaders recruited it's time to train them. You will find leaders have a greater sense of confidence if you spend time preparing them for the task you have recruited them to. It's important never to ask men to do something unless you can give them the training and tools necessary to do the job. There are a couple of things you can do to train men to be effective small group leaders:

Give your leaders a good small group experience of their own. The best way to train someone to be a small group leader is to have them be in a healthy small group themselves. We start in our recruiting and training by asking existing leaders who they have in their small groups that they feel would be good leaders in the future. Our leaders are always looking for the guy they believe they can disciple with the purpose of seeing him lead his own group in the future. If someone has seen modeled what it is to lead a discussion, handle a tough question, and tame the guy who talks all the time, he is far better prepared to lead than the guy who hasn't been in a group or the guy who has been in a dysfunctional group. Start by looking right under your nose—with the men in the groups.

Give your leaders an overview of the basics of small group ministry. You will want to have a time when you cover basic material on how to lead a group. You could have three consecutive Monday evening sessions or an extended session on a Saturday, or even one evening a month during the summer to train the leaders. We have done all three. They all have pluses and minuses. During these sessions we have tried to pass on the following information:

> The purpose of small groups
> Small group dynamics
> Communication skills—listening attentively and accurately, stimulating feedback
> How to study the Bible inductively
> How to lead a good discussion—asking good questions, keeping the discussion going, handling conflict
> How to start and finish a group
> How to choose members
> How to lead an effective prayer time
> How to handle difficult people or questions.

Training Session Tips

Some things that will help the training sessions:

1. *Give the men a good small group time.* The training in itself can be one more opportunity for your men to have a healthy group experience. Structure your training to accomplish some of the things you want your leaders to accomplish with their own groups. Give the men a chance to get to know

one another and to pray for one another.

2. *Give the men homework.* We had our men read through the *Brothers* book by Promise Keepers over the course of three weeks. We had them do an inductive Bible study and share their results with a small group. We then had them write five questions from that study, and finally had them actually lead a discussion on one of the nights.

3. *Make it practical.* Instead of simply imparting a load of information, we tried to give them on-the-job training, having them apply what they were learning. By having to lead a discussion, they took what they learned in the class and used it immediately. One thing that is helpful—and a hoot—during this time is to have a couple of "plants" in the group—a guy who won't stop talking, and another who asks the most bizarre questions you've ever heard.

4. *Allow plenty of time for questions.* For most of the men, leading a group is something new and they bring some fears with them. Allow them time to ask questions about what you discuss.

5. *Keep it simple.* Most men are bottom-line oriented. They don't care about the history of small groups or intricate theories of how or why they work. They want to know when to start, what to cover and how to do it. Stick to the basics. If you don't know where to start, most Christian bookstores have great material on leading small groups and training others to lead. Because of space I cannot include our entire training session.

Seven Small Group Decisions

Each small group faces seven decisions that determine much of the flavor of the group. Some of these questions you may have settled before you start training your men. Others you may sort through with your new recruits. Either way, your men need answers to these questions:

1. *What is our purpose?* The leader will in some way want

to advertise the group. He needs to be able to tell others what type of group he is starting. Is it a task group? An accountability group, study group, support group or hybrid group? He needs to be clear in his thinking on this one.

2. *Who should be in the group?* Is this group going to be an affinity group, with men in similar occupations to mine? Or will it be a diverse group? There are pros and cons to each. It really depends on what you want to do in the group. If you are looking to start an accountability group, you probably want an affinity group—guys you enjoy hanging out with who are experiencing the same pressures and stresses. Groups seem to jell easier at the start when the members are more or less at the same stage of life and at the same point in their spiritual journey.

3. *Will our group be open or closed?* Once the group is started will we allow new people into the group? Again this will be dependent on what the purpose of the group is. Men who want to join a sexual addiction support group need to be filtered through a group leader. Bible study groups may want to take new members when they reach a break in their material.

4. *When will our group meet?* Weekly? Biweekly? In the morning before work or in the evening after work—or during the Sunday school hour? I have seen that meeting every week helps to keep a group going. If a guy misses a meeting he doesn't have to wait so long to get back into the swing of things.

5. *Where do we meet?* For the group just beginning, a restaurant may be okay. Most restaurants have tables large enough to handle groups of five or more. They may even have private rooms where your group can meet alone. Restaurants, of course, also give the added opportunity for a good meal. Men love that. The downside is the noise and men's self-consciousness about talking through spiritual issues in a public place. It's tough to break into groups to spend a significant time praying and sharing in the middle of a restaurant.

An alternative is to bring in bagels, muffins, donuts and juice to a conference room at someone's office. Many of our groups meet in conference rooms around the community. Not only are these rooms usually quiet, they put the group on the men's turf. Another possibility is to have the group in someone's home. This works only if there is a rec room or study away from family.

6. *What commitment level do we expect?* Once a group has formed it's a good idea to develop a group covenant—to put down in writing what is expected of the members and what the group is about. Ownership is key. It may take one or two sessions to work it out, but you will find it extremely helpful down the road. I would encourage you to go back to the covenant on a regular basis—every three months—to remind yourselves of why you exist. A sample covenant appears at the end of this chapter.

7. *What are we going to study?* If your group will have a study component, you will need to decide that either as a group or ahead of time as the leader. In order to get guys started in groups you might need to address some of the hot men's issues, such as parenting, marriage, balancing work and home, to get them in. Once they're hooked you will want to move them to a more well-rounded study that includes studying Bible books and developing Christian disciplines.

Starting Groups at Your Church

The leaders are recruited. They're trained. They're ready to go. What lies ahead is the process of structuring the ministry and drawing men into the groups. The following tips might be helpful in this process:

1. *Find a coordinator for small groups.* Groups are such an important, integral aspect of ministry you will want one of the men on your leadership team to be in charge of this ministry. He should be someone with experience as a small group leader and have a vision for multiplying himself through others. He

should have, or work with someone who has, administrative gifts. Not only will he be responsible for training leaders but also for getting men into the groups—sharing that task with the group leaders. At times, group organization can be a time-consuming administrative nightmare.

2. *Designate shepherds for the small group leaders.* It's common for leaders to give to others but feel uncared for themselves. Either the coordinator or someone on his team should take the responsibility of caring for group leaders—praying for leaders often, calling them weekly or biweekly to see how they are doing and meeting with them a couple of times a year. We have found that a shepherd is able to oversee up to six leaders. More than that is overwhelming.

3. *Provide continuing education.* Assemble your leaders once a quarter to provide further training, share and pray for one another and discuss problems in the groups. A possible schedule would look like this:

7:00–7:15	Refreshments and catching up
7:15–8:00	Break into small groups to share and pray for one another
8:00–8:10	Break
8:10–8:30	Discuss any problems coming up in the groups
8:30–9:00	Teaching on a topic related to leading small groups

4. *Create windows for group start-ups.* Certain times of the year are better than others for starting small groups. Use some of the highlights of the year to get them going. An obvious time would be after a Promise Keepers Conference. At the conference your men will hear lots of encouragement to get into a small group. You might want to consider having a post PK event where men can sign up. Another good time would be your fall kickoff. By starting at this time you can publicize nine-month groups that run from September through May. You can use the summer to train leaders and then make a big push at the fall kickoff. One final time to start groups is after

a major special event—after a midyear retreat you probably will find men ready to join small groups. Remember to have those vital testimonies at every major event where a man tells how small groups have impacted him. Over a period of time your men will know when groups are likely to start and can look forward to that window of opportunity.

5. *Encourage your leaders and other men to get into an inviting mode.* Personal invitations are still the best way to get men into small groups. When we train our leaders we ask them to make a list of prospective participants and to start praying for them with the intent of asking them to join.

6. *Publicize the small groups.* One complaint you may hear from men is "I didn't know about the small groups for men." It really doesn't matter how many times you have said it—some people keep missing it. Your ministry brochure should list current small groups, with the time and place they meet as well as the group leader's name. Make sure you list the name and phone number of the person in charge of getting men into small groups—so that a man who is interested only has to make one call. Some churches have flyers with all the small groups listed—detailing when and where they meet, what they are studying and who to contact to join. These lists are great as long as they are kept current.

7. *Stay flexible.* After spending three years trying to match up men who wanted to be in small groups, we have altered our tactics. We have started telling our men that being in a small group is an option—but that we weren't going to do all the work for them. We told them to go out and form groups on their own. We encouraged them to find men who were similar in maturity, some who they had things in common with and who shared similar schedules. We provided a small group starter kit and told them to go to it. We asked only that they let us know when they had a group going.

It's remarkable to hear of all the groups that have started this way. This isn't to say we don't rely on training leaders and starting up official groups. But we realize that many men don't fit into the nice neat packages we develop, so we allow them to form their own groups, let us know what they're up to and whether they would like any new people to join them.

8. *Form small groups out of existing ministries.* Another way to start groups is to use what already works for you. Three ideas:

(a) *Committee groups.* Encourage working committees in the ministry to become a small group. I have twelve men responsible for the Top Gun ministry. These men meet weekly for two hours. Half the time is spent doing small group things, such as sharing, praying for one another and studying a variety of materials. The other half of the time is spent in business—developing the business plan for the ministry, setting goals, planning training sessions and making the ministry happen.

(b) *Monthly meetings.* Many of you already have a monthly meeting for the men of your church. Incorporate into those meetings times to break into discussion groups. Then you can encourage those groups to meet the other weeks of the month on their own.

(c) *Top Gun groups.* One of the purposes of the Top Gun ministry is to provide a catalyst for new small groups to start in the church. Every May when the groups finish their time together, we challenge them to stay together as a small group— a TG II group. They have already spent two hours a week together for nine months. Some serious male bonding has already transpired, so why not stay together? It's a way for us to start about ten new groups each year. Having been in a Top Gun group for a year, these men are fully convinced of the need to be in a men's small group for the rest of their lives.

9. *Be creative.* I could give you diagrams and charts of how this should all look but it wouldn't do you much good. The best thing you can do is sit down with your leadership team, take the basic principles described in this chapter and in other books and develop your own model for small groups. Again,

it comes down to what I said in the beginning: Each church is unique and the small group system will be unique as well.

Principles for an Effective Group

Finally, here are some points for your small group leaders to return to again and again to keep their groups sharp.

1. *Keep your focus.* Make sure you decide as a group up front what your purpose is. Stick to it. It will be easy to slide into other things and activities if you don't remind one another of why you meet. Is it to study, to pray, be accountable, or a combination?

2. *Start and finish on time.* One person in the group should be responsible to start the group on time and let everyone know when the time everyone committed to is up.

3. *Focus on people not programs.* It's easy to discuss deep subjects and to debate theological issues, and never get to matters of the heart. Start your group with plenty of time for group members to get to know one another. Schedule a night to socialize for this purpose.

4. *Move slowly.* Men don't easily open up the hurts, pains and frustrations of life. It takes time. For vulnerability to happen in your group, start by developing an environment of love and acceptance, not judgment. In order for accountability to happen, honesty and trust must be in place first.

5. *Take the lead.* Vulnerability is caught not taught. If you are frustrated because no one is sharing, take the initiative. Share what is going on in your life. Most men won't share fears, failures or feelings because they don't know how. They have never been in an emotionally safe environment. You take the lead.

6. *Live as a body.* Some of the greatest ministry will take place outside your group, when specific needs arise in the men in your group. Make yourselves available to help in times of need and feel free to call the others in your group for help.

7. *Keep discussions going.* When you discuss a chapter in

a book or a section of Scripture, there are three simple guidelines: Wait your turn. Stay on the topic. Keep it brief.

8. *Cultivate small group prayer.* The *ABCs* of small group prayer are: *Audible*, so all can hear. *Brief*, so that you do not take everyone else's time. And *Christ-centered*, so you don't spend all your time praying about Aunt Jane's ingrown toenail. If someone doesn't feel comfortable praying out loud, make sure he knows he doesn't have to.

9. *Avoid the known killers of small groups.* There are at least six ways to kill your group: aimlessness, poor leadership, the wrong mix of men, shallowness, individualism and competition. Be warned.

10. *Just do it.* Take these guidelines to heart, but plunge in and do small groups. They're the stuff of real Christian faith.

Exercise 2—Sorting Through Small Groups

1. How are you going to recruit and train men to be small group leaders?

2. What is your strategy to get men into groups?

3. What types of groups are you going to offer?

4. Who is going to oversee this aspect of the ministry?

5. What are the signs of a healthy men's group?

6. Are all the groups going to study the same thing or will each group study whatever they would like to study?

7. When is the best time to kick off the small group ministry?

Good Books on How to Lead Small Groups:

Brothers! Calling Men Into Vital Relationships, by Geoff Gorsuch, NavPress, Colorado Springs, Colo., 1994.

How Dynamic Is Your Small Group? by David Seemuth, Victor Books, Wheaton, Ill., 1991.

Getting Together, by Em Griffith, InterVarsity Press, Downers Grove, Ill., 1982.

The Big Book on Small Groups, by Jeffrey Arnold, InterVarsity Press, Downers Grove, Ill., 1992.

Example of a Small Group Covenant

1. *Total and complete confidentiality.* What you hear here, see here and say here stays here. I will say nothing that may be traced back or that could be injurious or embarrassing to my group members.

2. *Be as open as you can with your life.* I will be as open with my life at this time as I can. I will show myself to you, letting you know who I am as a person.

3. *Unconditional love.* I will love and affirm you no matter what you have said or done in the past. I will love you as you are and for what Christ wants to make of you.

4. *Voluntary accountability.* I will ask the group to hold me accountable for specific areas of my life. With my permission you can ask me about the goals I set with God, my family, personal life and world. I expect you to lovingly not "let me off the hook." "As iron sharpens iron, so one man sharpens another" (Proverbs 27:17). On the basis of this verse, I ask you to please share with me areas in my life that do not reflect Jesus, because I want to grow in personal holiness.

5. *Pray for one another.* I promise to pray for the men in my group on a regular basis, to lift up their needs to the Lord.

6. *Sensitivity to where people are at in the Lord.* I understand every person in this group is at a different point in their walk with the Lord. I will accept you the way you are, but encourage you to move on in the Lord.

7. *Come prepared each week.* I will have my work completed and my verse memorized each week when I come to class. I will make every effort to be present at class; it will have high priority in my schedule.

Signed _____

Date _____

Notes

1. Bill Hybels, on a tape series entitled, *Enlisting in Little Platoons*, Tape 1: "The Purpose of Little Platoons," 1989, Willow Creek Community Church, Barrington, Ill.
2. Howard Hendricks, on a tape given at Campus Crusade Staff Training at Fort Collins, summer of 1993, entitled "The Age of Accountability."
3. Chuck Swindoll, in a message given at the 1993 Promise Keepers Conference in Boulder, Colo.

Coaching the Leaders

It's a fall tradition in Madison. Coaches walk the lines at freshman orientation hunting tall, strong guys who don't play football—men between 6'2" and 6'6", 180 to 200 pounds, with strong backs, legs and arms and long endurance. It's a strange way to scout oarsmen for the University of Wisconsin crew team—to build what over the years has become a team heaped with tradition and national championships.

The recruits train constantly. Running miles and miles year-round, rowing in a tank all winter and out on the frigid lake as soon as the ice breaks in spring. Eight men sit on sliding seats facing the rear of the boat, feet strapped to the bottom of the shell, each manning one oar. There's a ninth man on the team: the coxswain. Usually about 5'4" and hopefully weighing not much more than 100 pounds, the cox sits in the back of the shell facing the oarsmen. Holding blocks of wood attached by ropes to the outside of the shell he beats out the cadence of the stroke. With these ropes he also works the rudder. Although he has to be small, the main requirement for a coxswain is a strong, deep voice. He yells out the pace, shouting instructions and encouragement to the team. He's the only one who can see where the boat is going and how the competition is doing. His job is to take the boat over the finish line having drawn the very best effort out of every man on the team and having kept them working together with such harmony that the boat nearly flies over the water. Although the cox never dips an oar into the water and the oarsmen constantly assure him that he is no more than a noisy irritation in the back of the boat, most admit he is the most indispensable member of the team.

Our role in ministry is like the coxswain. When you lead a men's ministry you need to keep looking ahead, giving direction, setting the pace, measuring the strengths and weaknesses of your team, keeping them pulling together and cheering them on. We're even more than coach and cheerleader rolled into one. We don't shout advice from the sidelines. We're out in the water with our team, urging them to give their best for the Lord.

In this chapter we will look at how you and I can lead others to the finish. How we coach men. How we lead leaders. How we ride "point." In my mind nothing is more exhilarating than leading. I want to pass on practical suggestions on recruiting, developing, training, shepherding and releasing others into ministry. At the end of the chapter I will again list some of the best books on this topic. But what I do want to do now is share five principles helpful in leading others.

Principle 1: Invest Your Life in Your Leaders

In 1 Thessalonians 2:8 Paul says this: "We loved you so much that we were delighted to share with you not only the gospel of God but our lives as well, because you had become so dear to us." Paul clearly says that the *goal* of his ministry was to share the Gospel, and down in verse twelve he says that the *outcome* of his ministry would be people who live lives worthy of the Gospel. But he also says he took great delight in sharing his *life* with the Thessalonians. Paul wasn't so goal-oriented that he lost sight of the real people he sought to impact. Paul realized that when he died he would live on in the men and women he had invested his life in. He understood that ministry was more than speaking a message—even the message of eternal salvation. It was also walking alongside the people God had entrusted to him. The principle I draw from this has become a cornerstone of my ministry among men: *The closer you get to the men, the greater the impact you will have on them—and the greater the impact they will have on others.*

One of the first books I received as a new Christian was Robert Coleman's *The Master Plan of Evangelism*,[1] a book I would recommend your leadership team read together. In this short paperback Coleman over and over again makes the point that the method of Jesus wasn't to worry about the masses but rather to invest three years of His life in the lives of twelve men. It was these men who in turn would reach the masses.

The principle stills holds today. It's easy to get sidetracked by the masses. But if we are going to be effective in leadership we have to decide early on that we can only work with so many people and that the best way to multiply ourselves is to pass on what we know and who we are to a few others. The great German theologian Dietrich Bonhoeffer, who spent months in a German concentration camp, penned these words: "The righteous man is one who lives for the next generation." One of my brothers put that statement on a plaque and hung it beside his bedroom door. Every day when he leaves the house he is reminded to pour his life into another.

I am no financial wizard, but my wife, Colleen, and her *Quicken* software keep things flowing along just great. Over the years, however, I *have* picked up a few simple things from friends and newspaper articles—and from my father-in-law. He is constantly handing me diagrams, illustrations and articles on the importance of packing in our money for the future. One principle he has driven home is the "magic of compounding." It's basically this: if you invest your money early and consistently, the interest you draw will go back into the pot. You earn interest on your interest—and that leads to a substantial growth in your savings. If you give the process time, the investment pays off many times over—like magic.

That principle holds true in Christian leadership as well. If early on in your ministry you take time to encourage, listen, teach and build up another man—and you stick with it over a long period of time—he will take all he has learned from you and multiply it into the next generation. In finances it's called the magic of compounding. In the faith it's called multiplication of life—through investing in others. In 2 Timothy 2:2 Paul instructs his young disciple, Timothy: "And the things you have heard me say in the presence of many witnesses," he says, "entrust to reliable men who will also be qualified to teach others." In this passage Paul describes a massive multiplication. He mentions four generations of people being influenced: Paul himself, Timothy and the other witnesses, reliable men, and the others they teach. An almost unbelievable payback!

Let me share some practical ways you can make heavenly investments in the lives of men you work with.

Demonstrate a Consistent Lifestyle

In the same way that small, consistent investments pay off financially, so the small, consistent influence of a godly lifestyle will pay off in the men you work with. In 1 Peter 5:2–3, it says we as leaders are to be "examples to the flock." In Philippians 3:17, Paul exhorts the Philippians to "join with others in following my example." There is no escaping this truth: one thing our society is looking for is leaders whose beliefs and behavior are congruent, whose actions are consistent with what they articulate, who make visual through their lifestyle what they verbalize with their lips. Give your men time to see you in the everyday aspects of life:

How you treat a slow server at a breakfast meeting.

How you exhibit patience when your little child runs up

to you in the middle of a conversation.

How you honor your wife in front of others.

Why you go to the Lord in prayer with your daily decisions.

What you are learning in your daily devotions.

How you respond to competition in the gym or watching a game.

You want your men to see what it looks like for a Christian man to do business, lead a family and seek after God. You want them to see you bring Christ into every aspect of your life.

Share Your Time

For a financial investment to grow it needs time. Putting money in a mutual fund for a few weeks, months or years won't do it. Multiplication takes many years. The same is true of relationships with men: they need time. Having meals together and going to games, retreats and planning sessions allows you to make small but necessary investments in their lives. It takes time to tear down the protective walls men build up around themselves.

I once heard Howard Hendricks explain that when he can't travel with his wife he always tries to bring one of his students from Dallas Seminary with him. He said the trips provide an opportunity to just hang out with a young man and to talk about everything under the sun. That priority has stuck with me. Whenever I go to speak at a church on a Sunday morning or to do a weekend retreat for another church I ask one of my leaders to come with me. I have found these travel times yield some of the best fellowship I have ever experienced. Something about being alone with a guy for a couple of hours allows the walls to come down and vulnerable sharing to take place. A number of my most significant discussions with men have taken place in that context.

Include others in what you are doing. Make spending time with men a habit.

Serve Men

The great UCLA basketball coach John Wooden said in his book *They Call Me Coach* that he would never ask his players to do anything he himself wasn't willing to do. The night before a game he would take his players to a hotel away from the campus so they could get a good night's sleep. But instead of going home to be with his wife, he would spend the night at the hotel with the players.

To serve another man is to invest in his life. It's interesting when you study Jesus' life to note that He too never asked the disciples to do anything He wasn't willing to do himself.

He asked them to pray and He prayed.

He asked them to serve and He washed their feet.

He asked them to love one another and He died on the cross for them.

The disciples learned from being with Jesus. From watching Jesus do the work of the Father. Christianity is contagious, more caught than taught. Christianity is like a fire. People see a fire and they want to be there to watch. They are intrigued by it.

When you are in the trenches serving your men they will catch your spirit. Remember? Jesus came not to be served but to serve and to give His life as a ransom for many (Mark 10:45). Many are into upward mobility. Jesus and His followers are into downward mobility.

I'm not saying that if you lead a men's ministry you have to be involved with *everything*. In fact, this book gives you tools to enable and empower others to do the work of the kingdom. What I am saying is that leadership isn't barking orders and sitting back and expecting others to do all the work alone. It isn't about lording your leadership over people, but rather serving them. Your men will see you serve when you help set up chairs before a meeting, when you help stuff a mailing that needs to get out, when you take a discussion group because a leader can't make it. If you make yourself available you will never lack opportunities to serve your men.

Shepherd Men

As you go along you will find different ways to care for the spiritual needs of your leadership team. We all have different gifts, so how you shepherd your men may look completely different from how other leaders shepherd. But some of the ways you can care for your guys are:

Pray for them regularly. Call them up or find out when you're together how you can pray for them. Let them know you've been thinking about them. I try to pray for two or three different leaders each day, so that over the course of a week I will have prayed for all of the guys I work with personally.

Keep your ears open. I am trying to develop an empathetic ear and heart. If I hear that life is going well for a man or that another man is struggling I call to see how things are going and find out if I can do anything to help. It's amazing how much you learn when you listen.

Get together with them. Get together one-on-one with your key men a few times over the course of the year just to talk. You may spend some of the time talking about the ministry—problems or ideas they need to talk through. But spend most of the time just asking how things are going. In Chapter 5, I listed a number of questions I ask my leaders, and you have freedom to go from there.

Send cards. Keep a stash of notes or stationery handy and you will be able to jot off a congratulations for birthdays or wedding anniversaries. If a man or his family is going through a tough time you can send an appropriate card. You're telling the men they are important and what they face is important to you as well.

Principle 2: Train Your Leaders

For many guys a huge roadblock to their serving in the church is their fear that they won't do the job right. Men fear failure, as we discussed earlier. A second key to working with your leadership team is providing the training men need to do what you have asked them to do. You squelch fears when you give men skills, instruction and resources to do the job properly. Here's the principle: *Never ask a man to do anything you aren't willing to train him to do.*

"Training" sounds like a weekend of sitting through boring seminar lectures. I have found that most of my effective training takes place in shorter, less formal settings. Here's a list of some ways you can train your men:

Train through small groups. By far the most effective training I have done has been through our Top Gun program. Training isn't the main purpose of the program, but throughout the course of the year I was able to share basic leadership principles and slowly drew along a number of guys based on their giftedness.

If you are just starting your ministry it may be hard to wait to begin small groups or a monthly meeting, but you can't go wrong taking your first year just to develop your leadership. You will set a solid foundation for whatever course you take in the future. And the best way to do that is to gather a group of men around you and meet as a small group. You don't have to use Top Gun. There are plenty of great leadership books out there that will help you prepare your men. It's sad that we have been deceived into believing that we can train hot men and women leaders as quick as we can scorch a cup of coffee in the microwave—we think that if we do the right conference or seminar, we can make instant leaders. It just doesn't work. It takes time.

Committee meetings. The normal give-and-take of a planning meeting almost always opens opportunities to interject good leadership principles. These are quick little minute-or-less lessons. During the meetings I often find myself coaching the men on church procedures—how to reserve rooms, get bulletin announcements and keep the custodial staff on our side.

Books. Another thing I like to do with my key coordinators is to read a book together, and then when we meet monthly we can take time to discuss it. Some books I have found helpful are *The Master Plan of Evangelism* by Robert Coleman, *Too Busy Not to Pray* by Bill Hybels, and *Hand me Another Brick* by Chuck Swindoll. Studying books together gives all the leaders a common understanding of service and ministry and it keeps them reading—which most men do not like to do. I do love to read and often pass on a good book when I finish it.

Resources. One way you can train your men informally is by providing them with resources. Besides books, you can use periodicals. You may want to get a subscription to *Discipleship Journal* for each small group leader. Ask your pastor to pass on good articles he comes across. Some video series make great take-home helps that men can view at their convenience.

Consulting. It's often helpful to bring in an outside person to meet with your leadership team. They can hear what you're doing and provide objective feedback.

On-the-job training. Whenever possible I work alongside another man first before asking him to do a job by himself. Our men do the same. On our special events committee, each member is grooming another man to take his place. These men attend all the meetings and take some responsibilities to prepare them to lead. With our Top Gun groups, any of the men can lead the group after the first three months, if they choose to do so. It's a nice safe environment in which to grow leadership skills.

Outside seminars and conferences. If you have men preparing to lead small groups, Serendipity provides regional training sessions that do excellent training. Promise Keepers holds their Leadership Conference across the country, and that would help other leaders. Your pastor probably has a handle on what training you have available in your area.

In-church training. This is supplemental to all the other types of training you provide. When you have informal training taking place, these sessions can be job-specific and relatively short. With our Top Gun program, a man must first have gone through the program as a participant before he can lead a group. Once through the group, he can take a three-night course to get the skills to lead a group with another man. We meet for three consecutive Monday evenings for two hours. We divide the time this way:

7:00–7:30	Teaching time—walk through the training manual
7:30–8:00	Small group discussion of the material
8:00–8:10	Break
8:10–8:40	Teaching time
8:40–9:00	Small group discussion of the material

If you are training men to lead small groups there are many ways to divide up your time. But keep the following points in mind:

1. Provide plenty of time for discussing the material.
2. Provide time for sharing and prayer.
3. Give them homework to read and complete between sessions.
4. Provide time during the sessions for men to lead what they are being trained to lead.

Principle 3: Create a Winning Environment for Your Leaders

I know even less about gardening than I do about finances. My personal gardening motto is this: I've never met a plant I couldn't kill. Nevertheless, every spring I go with my wife to the greenhouse to help pick out flowers. (She wants me to have a say in what I spend my summer killing.) For me the best part of that trip is the greenhouse. I love going inside and seeing those plants sprouting with incredible speed. The reason they grow so fast, of course, is that the greenhouse is an almost perfect environment for plants. The light, water, fertilizers and warm temperatures all work together to enable the plants to grow.

That's your goal at church. You want to develop an ideal environment where men can flourish in both growth and leadership. I feel fortunate to have spent twenty years in a feeding, nurturing setting. I have worked hard to create a similar environment for the men God entrusts to me. In this section I will share how you can develop a ministry where leaders are free to be all that God wants them to be—where they feel freedom to take risks, to grow, to step out and use the gifts God has given them. These are the environmental qualities you want to foster:

Give encouragement. Just as plants can't grow without a life-giving dose of water, people can't serve and lead without a life-giving source of encouragement. Encouragement can put a smile on the face of a child, lift the shoulders of a broken man, change the course of a young man's day, week, month and even his life. Without encouragement we shrivel and die.

You can encourage through *notes*. A quick note at the right moment to a man on your team takes a guy a long way. When I receive a note from our senior pastor or one of our senior associates I'm ready to sign up for another year of service. A note says I'm a valued part of the team and that they are interested in what I am doing.

You can encourage through a *word*. Whenever you get a chance, thank the men for all they do, for the sacrifices they make and for the impact they have on others' lives. A word spoken face-to-face will carry them a mile.

And you can encourage men through a *look*. I can still remember when I was in grade school playing for the divisional championship in baseball. I had just clobbered a game-winning home run and as I rounded second base I looked to the stands for my parents. My father—a very quiet man—just looked at me and gave me a nod of approval. His look said, "I am proud that you are my son." It's a look I will carry with me the rest of my life. You will have ample opportunities to give a look to another man that says, "thanks" or, "that was great" or, "I'm proud to be associated with you." When your men spend forty to sixty hours a week getting beat up at work and told they need to sell more, fix more and do more, they find life-changing encouragement when you make a place where they feel encouraged.

Allow freedom to fail. I have mentioned that Stuart Briscoe, our senior pastor, has a saying that is a watchword for our staff and the thousands who volunteer at Elmbrook. "If a job is worth doing," he says, "it's worth doing badly." Give your men freedom to fail. More than anything else you can do, it will allow them to take risks, to step out and discover their gifts—and to take personal ownership of the ministry. If a man has to continually glance over his shoulder to see if someone is stomping up behind him to tell him what a terrible job he is doing he will never reach his potential as a leader. His gifts will be wasted. When you give away responsibility you also give men the privilege of doing a job their way, with their unique style.

Recognize leaders. Everyone loves to be recognized for a job well done. Think of creative, meaningful ways to let men know they have done well and that you're glad they are on the team. One year I threw a catered appreciation dinner for leaders and their wives. Someone played the piano before and during the meal and then I introduced each man and described the contribution he had made to the team during the last year. Another year we had a simple evening of dessert and fellowship. Another ministry at our church cooked a Sunday brunch for leaders and their families—a great touch because the pastor who scrambled hundreds of eggs can't cook anything more complicated than toast. Use these moments to reiterate your vision and talk about where you are headed in the future.

Take leadership retreats. Getaways for your leadership team are fantastic vehicles for accomplishing a number of important goals—one of which is to help them feel important, needed and valued. Try to take your leadership team away once a year for a day or so to plan, pray, play. You will develop a greater sense of team, and by including your team in planning this retreat they will be more likely to open up and tell you what they feel the team needs most at the moment.

You can limit your retreat to your core leadership team or open it wide to all men in leadership positions. You can accomplish different goals with different types of retreats: A *training retreat* uses seminars and hands-on training to improve ministry skills. A *team building retreat* aims to build relationships between all team members. You can spend your time sharing, worshiping and playing together. A *planning retreat* is spent on evaluating where you have been, brainstorming where you want to go and planning how to get there. Check back to Chapter 6 and Appendix B for hints on holding retreats.

Build a sense of team. Throughout this book I have purposely used the word "team" to describe the men who work with me in leadership. For me this is both natural and important. My leaders will blossom when they are all working toward the same goal and aren't interested in who gets the glory. The 1995 Packers are a great illustration. The previous year they lost one of their best players to a play-off injury. This past year—minus this supposedly key player—they were a much better team. Why? Chemistry. Any coach knows that chemistry or the lack of it can make or break a team. When you look for men to serve on your ministry start with men who have servant hearts and are willing to do anything for the cause. Build on that by providing ample time in your meetings for talk and prayer. Keep reminding them of the common vision and keep their collective eyes focused on Jesus.

Grow love and acceptance. Last and most important for creating a winning environment for your leaders: men take off when they realize they are accepted for who they are, not just what they can do. If encouragement is water, then love is the sun. Love takes phone calls any time of the day or night. Love gets excited about the things friends get excited about. Love listens to a man as he shares a wound he has carried for forty years. Love sees potential in others. Love believes that God can use a man and his gifts to make a difference in the kingdom. Love picks men up when they fall. Love feels as others feel.

Love. Pour it out on your men.

Principle 4: Give Away the Ministry

In the movie *Miracle on Ice*, the story of the 1980 U.S. Olympic hockey team, one of the most interesting scenes happens right after Herb Brook's American squad beats the Russians in the semifinals of the medal round. Players on the ice hug each other, others cry out of ecstasy, flags wave everywhere and the Lake Placid crowd chants *U.S.A.! U.S.A.!* Then there's a shot of Brooks. An assistant coach tells Brooks to get out on the ice with the guys to celebrate one of the greatest upsets of all time. Herb looks at his assistant. "This is their time of glory," he says. "They earned it. Let's let them enjoy it." Brooks turns his back and walks off to the locker room.

Real leadership gets excited seeing *others* succeed. It pulls together a group of men, equips them, trains them and then releases them to do ministry. Your ministry will only develop and grow as you develop leaders and allow them freedom. As long as you try to do everything yourself the scope of your men's ministry will be small and its impact limited. I want to give you basic principles for giving away the ministry—how to delegate to the men you coach.

1. *Point people in the right direction.* Planning is an overlooked process—which is why I have talked so often about it in this book. Your first task as a leader or leadership team is to decide what you want to do. Vision is deciding where you are going with the ministry and discerning what has to happen for you to get there. As a leadership team, for example, we have decided to add one new ministry every year until we get everything going that we feel God has called us to do. There are times I would like to do more and other times I feel our

goal is too high. But try hard to look out into *your* future. You have to know where you want to take your men.

2. *Transfer ownership.* You may be sure where your group should head. But you can't get your men anywhere without help. You need to give your men the authority, freedom and resources they need to perform as God has gifted them. Biblical delegation starts a man with small tasks, then moves him on to bigger assignments when he proves himself faithful. I start by putting men in charge of *things*, then move them to *projects*, and finally to *people*. Since people are our most precious commodity I want to make sure the guys we choose to lead them are men of character and ability.

You have to consciously work to give away ministry. Your first step to letting go is to make known what you need and expect. If I were going to get a man to head up a fall kickoff, I would sit down with him and go over the following:

What has to be done. I would cover the person's job description to ensure we are both thinking the same thing.

How it will be done. Greg Groh of Worldwide Leadership Council gave me a great suggestion a couple of years ago in this area. He told me to have a man make a list of everything that has to be done for the project or job he has to do. Then we take the list and label each task with a 1, 2 or 3. A "1" means he doesn't have to check with me to do the task. Most jobs fall into that category. A "2" means to go ahead and do it and tell me how it went. A "3" means he needs to talk with me first. This process is clear. It's simple. And it makes us partners.

When it will be done. I find it helpful to work with a man to develop a timeline for the area he is working on—not just a final date but intermediate checkpoints as well. For that fall kickoff we would set dates for getting help, scheduling a speaker, getting brochures out and more.

Who will help. This part of the discussion hammers home the fact that a guy almost always needs help to get the job done. I suggest names of potential recruits. I let him know how

I can be a resource to him. In the case of the fall kickoff, he would need men to take charge of publicity, program, registration, facilities, prayer and budget.

3. *Release your leaders.* In the summer of 1995, I served with Greg Groh on a leadership school in the Middle East. We worked with pastors, evangelists, church planters, counselors—all of whom were working in difficult situations. As we taught on prayer, discipleship, evangelism, planning worship services and other issues we used a phrase that has stuck with me: "catch and release." Leadership means helping men to *catch* a vision for using their gifts and then *releasing* them to do it.

I will tell you up front that when you give a job away your men won't do it like you would. They won't avoid the mistakes you would have seen a mile away. And they may never do their job as well as you could. But that's okay. Ministry isn't about perfection. It's about people—developing them into the men God wants them to be.

Releasing men is hard. It's also one of the most exciting things you will do as a leader. Tomorrow morning I will speak at our monthly breakfast. All I have to do is show up and speak. A team of twelve men has planned the meeting. They will greet the men, emcee the event, cook the food, lead the music, and guide the table discussions. I feel like a proud parent. Those twelve guys understand what ministry is and they are doing it. What excitement!

4. *Stay in touch with your leaders.* You need to be available to meet with the men to talk through how they are doing.

One of the problems with delegation is the "dump and run" phenomenon. A leader gives away an aspect of the ministry and then never makes progress checks, never offers follow-up help. As you give away your ministry, be available to support and encourage your hard-working men. What each man needs will be different. Some like a lot of room. They run with a job and forget all about you. Others need more time. You will learn how to best support your leaders as you get to know them. Be bold. Ask them to define what they must do to make their project successful. Make them tell you what you can to do help.

Principle 5: Organize the Ministry

The word "organization" evokes one of two reactions. For some, organization ranks right up there with root canals. For others it's sheer delight—and the more graphs, charts and systems the better. Wherever you may fall on the continuum one thing is certain. To grow your ministry you need to *plan* for growth and *structure* all you do in a way that facilitates growth, keeping in mind that the church is a living organism, not an organization. Here are some guidelines to help you assemble your ministry in such a way that the fire keeps burning and is not put out by the water of organization.

1. *Clearly define areas of responsibility.* I will say it again. Job descriptions ensure that your men know exactly what you need from them and what doing a job well involves. A proper job description includes the responsibilities to be carried out, the time frame for finishing, who to report to and the resources available to do the job well. Job descriptions provide a man both freedom and direction and make him accountable for clearly stated duties.

2. *Clearly define areas of care.* If your men are going to invest time, money and energy into ministry they need leaders who care for them while they do ministry. The privilege of serving shouldn't be an invitation to dry up and blow away. One mistake that is easy for your leadership team to make is to give a man responsibility and authority but fail to give him the support he needs. Build into your structure men whose job it is to care for the personal needs of leaders. If you have ten small group leaders in your ministry, have one man for every five leaders. Your encourager can call his men regularly, pray for them, help solve their problems and dream up new ideas with them. They can also watch for leader burnout.

3. *Evaluate whether your structure accelerates or hinders ministry.* Organizations can get so complicated that people spend more time working through the bureaucracy than actually doing ministry. I know plenty of ministries where people spend more time in meetings than they do out with their people. Discuss this fine balance as a leadership team and be willing to revamp your ministry offerings, to revise who does what and who answers to whom. What works for you the first couple years of your ministry may not work in year four. Adding more leaders and coordinators will certainly mean you need to make changes. Failing to adjust will choke your ministry.

Don't expect men to attend an endless number of committee meetings. Streamline as much of your work as you can through phone conferences and fax machines.

4. *Develop a model that works for you.* There are as many ways to structure a ministry as there are ministries. What works for someone else's ministry may not work for yours. Have some of your organizational types talk through what might work best in your unique situation. Here are some models I have seen function well in churches I have worked with.

When the pastor is responsible for the men's ministry

In this setup the pastor's main responsibility is overseeing the key coordinators and leaders. He sets the vision and provides leadership to those men.

A meeting every six or eight weeks pulling together the pastor and coordinators of major areas of ministry gives an opportunity for everyone to share what they see going on in their areas, to pray for one another and their ministries, and to plan for the future.

As I mentioned earlier in the book, I recommend co-coordinators. It's a structure that furthers teamwork, spreads responsibility and builds in accountability.

Each coordinator develops a team of men to do ministry in

their area of responsibility. The coordinators of our Top Gun program work with a larger team of ten men. They meet weekly to nurture one another and to plan and carry out the ministry. A special events coordinator, in contrast, may get his committee together only once a month, mostly to plan the upcoming event. How often and how long a team meets can be different for each area.

When the ministry is run by men working under a pastor

This situation assumes that the group's pastor is responsible not only for the men's ministry but a dozen other areas. In practice the ministry is run by one or two men who pull in others to help them do the work.

If this working committee has four to six guys, each can take a specific area of the ministry and develop a team of guys to work in that area.

The committee needs to meet every four to six weeks to discuss the various areas as well as to plan and pray.

The pastor needs to decide which of the committee meetings to attend, and the committee needs to decide how to keep him up to date if he chooses not to attend.

When just one man is enthused about a men's ministry

In some churches it may be only one man who is really excited about seeing something happen among the men at his church.

He should first talk to the pastor for his input.

He will need to be careful not to attempt too much and set himself up for burnout. As he moves ahead and desires to develop ministries he will need to coax others to help.

Most of this men's ministry will be informal, especially in the beginning—just meeting with men to encourage them and to spur them on in their walk with Jesus.

5. *Organize around weakness.* One final point. As you begin to determine the structure of your ministry, remember to

evaluate your team's strengths and weaknesses. As you consider which men in your church to approach to help in your ministry, think about which ones best make up for your weaknesses. I am a visionary who loves to be out in front of the men leading the charge. I am weak in my grasp of details. I overlook smaller steps we need to take to get us to the destination. I also consider myself a weak shepherd. I need men on my team who are detail-oriented and others who can shepherd the men. Get to know yourself and the men on your committee. Ask yourselves what you need to round out your team.

Notes

1. Robert Coleman (Old Tappan, N.J.: Fleming H. Revell Co., 1963), p. 21.

Special Teams

Special teams make or break a football team. A fumbled punt, a blocked field goal or a kickoff returned eighty yards for a touchdown can all change the complexion of a game. But special teams are often the part of the game coaches overlook, scrimping on time and effort. But here's a point too good to miss: when I coached ball and broke films down play by play I found that almost a third of the action in any game involved special teams. Special teams done right can impact enormously the score at the end of the game.

Special teams have the same big effect on a ministry. Mission teams and evangelism teams and other outreach specialties add excitement, diversity and depth to your ministry. "As air is to fire," Stuart Briscoe says, "so missions is to the church." Special teams may not be where you want to start, but you won't want to neglect them as time goes on.

Vacations With a Purpose

We like to call our ministry trips "vacations with a purpose." Having personally taken groups to the Philippines, Romania and Russia and planned for teams going many other places, I have seen firsthand the benefit a one- to four-week trip has for an individual, a ministry and the whole local church. I want to give you in this section some basic guidelines on carrying out short-term mission trips. We will cover the purpose for a trip, different types of trips you can take, planning a trip, trip recruiting and training, and the keys that make trips work.

Why Take a Trip?

Men work hard. They assume that the best way they can use time off from work is to hit the golf course or to head off to fish or hunt. Yet the incredible power of mission trips refresh both the server and the served.

1. *Mission trips expose men to the realities of life in another culture.* A ten-minute walk in the squatter slums of Manila teaches men that everyone doesn't live like we do. Watching gypsies driving horse-drawn carriages through the Carpathian Mountains of Romania reminds us that not many enjoy the conveniences we do. Seeing food lines string out block after block in Moscow, men realize that not everyone eats the way we do. Comfortable men in nice suburban settings don't realize that two-thirds of the world lives in utter poverty, disease and hopelessness. Taking people into these situations shocks them into reality. It forces them to deal with long-buried issues: *What is my responsibility? How can I help? How can I simplify my lifestyle? Where is God in all of this? Why has my country been blessed as it has?* National Geographic or a PBS special can give men the images, but a mission trip lets them pick up the smells, sounds and emotions of life on the other side of the planet.

A mission trip also enables men to start to see the world as God does. They see the suffering and injustice present in our world. They begin to notice the four billion people on this earth who don't know Jesus. It's an eye-popping experience.

2. *Mission trips give men a chance to see what cross-*

cultural missions is all about. We make sure our men understand that they are *not* missionaries—at least not in the sense of a cross-cultural worker who trains, prepares and then goes long-term to another world.

These trips indeed give men a chance to do real ministry. They watch and work alongside missionaries, getting a peek at their lives. Whenever possible we like our teams to stay in or close to the homes of the missionaries we work with. They see that doing the laundry isn't a two-hour job and that cooking often involves going to a morning market and spending a good part of the day preparing food. Trips help men grasp what it takes to work with people from another culture—people with different values and ways of doing things. It lets them see the extremely difficult situations missionaries work under and the sacrifice their families make for the cause of Christ.

3. *Mission trips let men assist in the work of Christian ministry.* Later we will discuss the types of trips you can take with your men. No matter what type you choose, though, you get the chance to encourage, support and strengthen the work missionaries are doing. Lack of money or personnel or time almost always curtails some of what missionaries would like to do. Having a well-prepared team come from your church can get things done in a short time that may otherwise never happen. If a missionary family needs an addition on their home, church or school, your church could raise the money to send the men to build it. If an outlying area lacks doctors you could send a couple of doctors and nurses to give physical exams—likely to children who have never seen a doctor in their life. One of our prerequisites for sending a team of men is that it must in some way further the ministry of one of our Elmbrook-sponsored missionaries. We aren't interested in just sending teams to do projects. We want to connect with our missionaries and be a vital part of what they are trying to do.

4. *Mission trips stretch men spiritually.* One of my friends who went on our last Philippines trip said he would only be able to take part if God sent the $2,000 necessary for the trip.

He watched in amazement as God provided exactly what he needed in a variety of ways. What a faith builder! John had never spoken a word in front of a congregation. When he arrived in Kabankalan—on the island of Negros—he was asked to preach on a Sunday morning at one of the forty-five outreach churches in the mountains. What made the challenge even greater was the fact that the invitation to preach came *after* he had arrived for the service that morning. He prayed fervently at the back of the sanctuary during the first half of the service—and then did a great job of sharing God's Word.

Everything that happens on a "vacation with a purpose" trip is the undoing of a "comfortable" faith. Financial concerns, culture shock, time changes, simple living situations, loneliness, busyness, hard work, detailed preparations—they all force a man to become more dependent on the Lord, more fired up for God.

The other ingredient in such a trip is the effect on your men of seeing the church in action in other parts of the world. In many ways the church in America is weak and sick compared to the church in other cultures, where it is generally much more vibrant and alive. Men go to Asia or Africa or South America to worship and pray and fellowship with men and women whose faith does not display the shallowness they often see in American Christianity. When I taught a leadership school in the Middle East this past year, it wasn't uncommon to hear men express their fear of being shot or imprisoned for their faith. Who would not be challenged by this? In Romania we attended worship services that lasted three hours. We caught a real glimpse of the people's love for God. In the Philippines we saw Christians gather at 5:00 A.M. morning after morning to pray for the people of the church and for the island outreach. Maybe that's why they have planted forty-five churches.

I think by now you get my point. I am convinced that these types of trips transform the lives and hearts of men and provide real service to the missionaries and nationals on the field.

Types of Trips

You can dream big when you think of the types of trips you can plan for the men of your church. You can wrap some of the following ideas together to accomplish two or three purposes on a given trip. On our last trek to the Philippines, we did both construction and medical work. These obviously aren't the only jobs to be accomplished, but they get you thinking of some possibilities:

1. *Construction trips.* This week we sent eight men to Venezuela to do construction work at a retreat center for pastors and missionaries in that country. Not the most glamorous trip in the world, but very necessary and greatly appreciated by the missionaries. You could put an addition on a school, church, house or hospital. You might cut down trees to carve out a landing strip in the Brazilian jungle. Whatever the project, it's a chance for men to help in the work of the kingdom.

Work teams range from one man going to help with a smaller project to a large number of men going to blitz the larger jobs. Last fall a carpenter went to Papua New Guinea for a month to help build a furniture-making shop and to train nationals to build furniture. Last year a Presbyterian church in Chicago sent twenty-five men to Mexico for a week to help construct modular homes. One great aspect of construction projects is that not everyone has to be a tradesman to be involved. A willing heart to do whatever has to be done makes a man a candidate for a construction team. There's always dirt to shovel, concrete to mix, lumber to move and walls to be painted.

Keep in mind:

Don't miss an obvious point: Do have a person on the trip thoroughly skilled in whatever the main purpose of the trip is—electrical work, plumbing, masonry, etc.

Find out early on exactly what is involved in the project and whether or not you will need to pay for the materials.

Try to get blueprints ahead of time so you can head off any problems.

Double-check on what tools are available and what you will need to bring along.

Get your non-construction guys in shape before you leave. There's nothing like mixing cement for ten hours a day in ninety-degree heat when all you normally do is sit at a desk.

2. *Medical trips.* The need for medical help in developing countries is incredible. Dentists, pediatricians, nurses, surgeons, dental hygienists, physical therapists—all are needed in various parts of the world. We have had dentists and surgeons go to Ghana to work with Prison Fellowship in that country's prisons. Pediatricians have worked in the Philippines with kids who have never seen a doctor. Surgeons have done reconstructive surgery in South American jungles and nurses have provided care in a Haitian orphanage—all in the name of Jesus.

Most churches won't be able to field an entire team of medical personnel. You can nevertheless get your healthcare professionals aligned with one of many medical missions agencies. They continually organize efforts all over the world. They have vast experience that helps to ensure all the supplies are present and pre-screening has taken place.

Keep in mind:

Will the supplies you need be on site or should you bring all of your own?

Do your people need any special licensing to do medical work in your target country?

Do you need to complete any special forms to get medicine through customs?

Will the sight be adequately staffed? What specialties are needed? Will there be an anesthesiologist, surgical nurse, etc.?

Who will pre-screen patients before you arrive? Your trips will be infinitely more productive if you can get right at your work.

You will need the best language interpreter you can get if you will be seeing patients.

3. *Athletic trips.* One of the simplest and most effective me-

diums for doing evangelism in other parts of the world is sports. Whether it's basketball, soccer, volleyball or baseball, sports are a universal language. Again, a number of agencies specialize in sending sports teams all over the world. Last year we sent nine men to Guatemala on an eight-day, twelve-game ministry trip. They went from town to town playing the local all-stars and semi-pro teams. At half-time they shared testimonies and a Gospel message. In parts of the world like South America and Asia it isn't uncommon to have two to five thousand people attend a game of this sort. If you have men in your group who are athletically inclined, this is a great way for them to spread the Good News. One of our Philippines teams saw so many people in a small barrio become Christians that the local church who sponsored us doubled in size.

Keep in mind:

Who in the host country will set up all the games ahead of time?

Is the schedule realistic for your men?

Allow a day for the guys to get accustomed to the climate.

Will there be a sound system, or do you need to bring one? Don't underestimate the number of spectators. You want your half-time message to be heard.

What level of competition can you expect? Make sure you are evenly matched with the people in the host country.

4. *Business trips.* Some guys may want to take part in a mission trip, but they aren't athletically, medically or mechanically inclined. I mentioned earlier that a couple of years ago I took three businessmen to Romania to set up a clothing resale shop intended to underwrite a small church. It was one of the most exciting trips I have ever taken. I saw these astute businessmen use their God-given gifts to teach how to brainstorm, strategize, market, budget—everything necessary to start up a small business. Another one of our men, who is a farmer, recently spent three weeks in Africa helping the local people with irrigation and cattle-raising skills.

Keep in mind:

Are you going as Western world know-it-all imperialists—or servants of God and man?

What do you know about the country's economy and business practices? *Know* before you go.

What cultural differences can you expect that will impact how you do business?

Who do you know who can coach you in legal and procedural issues?

Will you have language interpreters available who know business terms?

5. *Prayer trips.* When I first talked to our men about a prayer trip their first reaction was, "What are we going to build?" "What are we going to fix?" Right now I am planning a trip with four or five men to three world-class cities in a country relatively closed to the Gospel. We will spend three days in each city walking the streets and praying for the people. The Christian workers in these cities believe that some of the spiritual strongholds will only be broken down through prayer. And until this is done, the Gospel will not be received. This may not sound like a normal mission trip, but prayer is where the real battles are won for eternity. Prayer trips deepen the prayer lives of the men who go and of the people who send them.

Keep in mind:

You need to do a great deal of study ahead of time on the cities you will pray for—religious background, culture, societal issues, politics and so on.

Team members must not be new Christians, but men who are real prayer warriors and who already have a ministry of intercession at home.

Team members should gather a prayer team to pray for them back home while they battle in prayer in these closed cities of the world.

Team members need to be versed in spiritual warfare.

Team leaders should have a working knowledge of the cities that will be visited.

6. *In-country ministry trips.* You don't have to leave this country to experience another culture or to help the cause of Christ. You could, for example, take a group of men to minister to the rural poor in the Appalachians, or the urban poor in any major city in this country. Plenty of Christian organizations need help restoring buildings. And many summer camps could use a group of men to help with building projects or general grounds maintenance. These domestic trips can be shorter in length—even a weekend—and usually considerably less expensive, making them a great way for many guys to get started.

Keep in mind:

What type of experience would be most beneficial to the men in your church?

What type of preparation does the organization provide, or what will your group need to do by way of preparation?

How to Plan a Mission Trip

In this section I will provide the basic steps to planning a short term mission trip for your men. There are at least a couple of good books that go into much more depth than I can here. *Vacations With a Purpose*[1] has great material and checklists for putting a trip together. *Stepping Out: A Guide to Short-Term Missions*[2] is also a good guide for your planning and team training.

Getting Started

1. *Determine where you want to go and what type of trip you should take.* Go to these three resources to get info on potential projects, in this order:

Your pastor. Ask him if your church has any missionaries looking for help. If he is unaware of any current needs you could ask him for a mailing list of missionaries supported by your church and then send them a letter to request information directly.

The second source is *your missions committee*, if your church has one. The committee coordinator should be able to detail some of the needs of the agencies and missionaries they work with.

The third source would be *your denominational missions headquarters*. Often they organize projects all over the world that you can tie in to. Trips sponsored by a denomination are a great place to start because they do the logistical work for you and you wouldn't need to field a whole team from your church to make it happen.

I am not against working with other organizations that send men on trips all over the world. My first choice, however, would be to link up with missionaries connected with your church. If your church has taken on obligations of prayer and funding for a particular project or missionary family, a mission trip to help out is a natural for everyone involved.

Besides determining what type of trip to take, you will need to decide the cost, location and length of it. An in-country trip is by far the easiest and least expensive. Going to Central or South America or Canada is relatively inexpensive and still leave you the option of going for just one week. Some things to keep in mind as you make these decisions:

How long can your guys be gone from work?

How much do you think they can reasonably raise for the trip?

What connections do you as a church have with missionaries and mission agencies?

How many men do you think would be interested the first time around?

2. *Develop a budget.* Once you have fixed your dates and location, your next step is developing a trip budget. Budgeting will be done for you if you go with your denomination or a mission agency. These are some of the costs you can expect:

Travel
    Round-trip airfare
    In-country flights/transportation

Daily transportation (from place of lodging to work site)

Airport taxes

Food and Lodging

Cost per day for lodging

Cost per day for food

Extra hotel and meal costs while entering and leaving country

Training Materials

Team retreat

Reading material

Training manual

Miscellaneous Costs

Passports

Shots

Photography

Printing and postage for team

Money for building, medical, or athletic supplies

With a price determined you can start recruiting team members and put together a timeline.

3. *Plot a timeline for the trip.* This process may seem tedious but you will suffer needless headaches if you don't plan ahead. If you start doing things far enough ahead you won't be overloaded in the final few weeks before the trip. This is a bare bones timeline—you will need to fill in the gaps based on your trip, church and style:

Eight months before trip

Establish a planning committee

Determine when and where the trip will be

Begin to develop a budget for the trip

Six months ahead

Begin advertising the trip—prepare a brochure, hold an informational meeting, etc.

Arrange for transportation

Choose team leaders

Five months ahead
 Finalize your team
 Work with hosts on final arrangements
Four months ahead
 Begin training classes
 Apply for passports
 Plan fund-raising activities
Three months ahead
 Continue training classes
 Send out prayer and support letters
 Hold a pot-luck dinner for families
Two months ahead
 Go on a team retreat
 Do job-specific team training (bricklaying, basketball prac-
  tice, etc.)
 Visa applications should be in
One month ahead
 Get immunizations
 Confirm flights and other travel arrangements
 Have a send-off at your worship service
 Get traveler's checks for your team

This isn't an exhaustive list but it gives you an idea of what you might need to include on your own timeline.

4. *Recruit team members.* It's one thing to draw up plans for a trip. It's another to convince others that it will be good for them to go. To be honest, it can be tough the first time. Once you have a history of trips and can show videos and share testimonies from former team members it gets easier—especially if the trip was a positive experience! While it's the job of everyone on the planning committee to help recruit team members, you may want to have one man oversee your efforts. Some recruiting tactics:

Brochures. Include the date, destination, what you will do, your purpose, cost, team leader, basic schedule, date of informational meeting, expectations and application. I have found it helpful as part of the application process to have men write a one-page letter explaining why they want to go on the trip. You may want to include a map of the country where you will work to give people a better idea of where you are going.

Informational meetings. After the brochures and bulletin announcements have been out for a month or so, hold an informational meeting. This is your chance to describe the trip in greater detail, maybe to show a video or slides from previous trips and to have a couple of men share testimony regarding their experience on a short-term project. Make sure to leave plenty of time for questions and get a list of all the men who attend so you can follow them up.

Bulletin blurbs. Use every means available to you to advertise the trip. Make sure your trip is in the bulletin, church newsletter and any other information system available at your church.

Former team members. These men are usually a great means of recruiting others for a trip. Once we schedule a trip I usually contact all our former team members so they can start talking it up in their sphere of influence. They may also be potential team leaders.

Prayer. As the leader of our men's ministry I am always listening and looking for men who need to take the next step in their Christian development. I keep those men in mind during my prayer time and ask God to help us know if this trip would be a good thing for them. Your planning committee should spend time praying that God would raise up just the right men for the trip.

5. *Decide on the team.* This can be tricky. It helps if you are frank all through the publicity process that men need to apply and be accepted for the trip. Set a deadline for applications and know ahead of time whether you plan to take pretty much everyone who applies or a just a few men. The sorting process also works best if your planning committee determines some objective means for choosing or excluding

men—instead of leaving everything to subjective factors such as friendships and favorites.

Once you have received everyone's application, have your pastor look them over for any problems he might see. He may be aware of issues that would disqualify a man from going. Keep in mind the following issues when you make your selections:

Has the man been on a previous trip? You might need experienced men on this one. Or you might want to open up opportunities to new men.

Does he get along with others applying for the trip? Is there a good team fit?

Is he spiritually and emotionally mature enough to handle the trip?

Is he looking to serve—or simply wanting a chance to travel?

Do you have enough skilled men in the project area? This needs to be a priority.

6. *Train the team.* With the team selected it's time to prepare them for the trip. From a perspective of growing the participants, I use the trip as dessert—and the preparation time as the real meat of the trip. Several years ago we were preparing a group of two dozen college students to go to the Philippines on a combination music/basketball/child evangelism/construction project. We had spent two months meeting weekly together. We had a wonderful weekend retreat. Two weeks before our departure date there was a coup attempt in Manila and all travel from the United States was stopped. Without hesitation, all of the team members said that even if they didn't go, their efforts were worthwhile because of the growth that had taken place in their lives. The good news is that the coup attempt failed and we were able to go anyway. What an experience for these young men to see tanks, armored vehicles and soldiers everywhere they looked!

In order for your training to be effective there are a couple of things you will want to do.

1. *Training classes.* Six to eight weeks of classes work best. These shouldn't be solely sit-at-a-table-and-take-notes types. Include time for sharing and prayer, teaching and discussions of how to handle the practical aspects of the trip. In your teaching time you will want to cover the following subjects:

Week One   Devotions and prayer
Week Two   Testimonies—how to put one together and how
               to give one
Week Three   The biblical base of missions
Week Four   The biblical base of missions (cont.)
Week Five   Team building/relationships
Week Six   Culture shock
Week Seven   How to be a world-class Christian
Week Eight   Packing

Give homework that matches the topic of the week. Some books that may be good for your team to read over the course of the training would be *In the Gap* by David Bryant,[3] *Unveiled at Last: God's Call to Be Involved in World Evangelism Throughout the Bible* by Bob Sjogren,[4] or *Run With the Vision* by Bob Sjogren and Bill and Amy Stearns.[5]

2. *Team retreat.* To get away to a retreat center for a day or two really helps the walls come down within the team. It also helps them get used to living together in close quarters. If you have a ropes course or adventure course nearby, it is a great way to accelerate the team-building process. You can also do some team building exercises on your own at the retreat center—ask your youth pastor or sponsors for ideas. The retreat should also provide extended times of sharing, worship and prayer together. By this time a question like, "What was the most embarrassing moment in your life?" should go over well. Since you will be going as servants, I found doing a foot-washing service at the conclusion of the retreat to be memorable.

3. *Family pot luck.* A month or so before you leave you might want to gather all the team members and their families for a meal. It gives the wives a chance to meet the other wives

and to swap phone numbers so they can call each other for emotional support or practical help during the trip. It gives kids a chance to see slides of where Dad is going and, better yet, to hear from others *why* he is going. If you have people in your church or community from the country where you will work, you might want them to come and share about their country and what the men will experience there.

4. *Background research.* It's important for your team members to learn as much about the country as possible before you leave. Have them go to the public library and check out books and videos on that country, read and watch and then report back to the team. If there are language tapes available for your country, get those and learn some basic words.

Stress from the beginning that you are all going as learners and not as experts. When you learn about a country, you are telling the people that they are important and that their country is important. It says, "I care about you, your background, your struggles." By trying to learn the language and using it when you arrive—no matter how poorly—you say, "I am willing to humble myself and learn from you." This is the attitude you will want to foster among team members.

Ten Keys to a Successful Trip

You can know how to make a trip happen without knowing how to make it happen *well*. Here are some vital points to making it work:

1. *Flexibility.* "Roll with it" is the motto of any mission trip. Most of us like things to be structured—with some semblance of order and time. Life doesn't work that way in most countries around the world. Planes, buses and trains don't leave on time, church services start late and run long, times and schedules constantly change. You'll never know when you might be asked to give a word of testimony or bring a message. Drill into your team members the need to be flexible.

2. *Prayer.* The real battles are fought in the heavenlies. As

a result it's imperative to have an army of people praying for the team while you are away. I encourage each team member to find five other men who will commit to pray for them every day they are gone. You could also set aside a room on the Sundays the team is away for family members and friends to gather to pray for the team. You can develop prayer cards with prayer requests and a picture of the team.

3. *Spiritual readiness.* If a team expects to see fruit on the field they must be spiritually strong going into the trip. It is easy as the trip draws closer for the men to worry about all the packing and physical things that need to get done and to forget about preparing their hearts. Jesus tells us in John 15 that there is a direct relationship between abiding in Him and bearing fruit. Anything you can do to keep the men close to Jesus will help.

4. *A servant heart.* I have said it already but I want to say it again. Your men need to see themselves as servants to the missionaries and to Christians and non-Christian nationals, not as saviors from the West. The nationals smell arrogant foreigners an ocean away. The greatest compliment you could ever receive is for people to say you were humble and served well. When you work with men it isn't hard to find out who has or doesn't have a servant heart. You want guys on your team who are willing to do anything, not those who want their pillows fluffed and their egos stroked.

5. *Team building.* The more you can do the better. Harsh environments bring selfishness to the surface. The chaos and rustic living conditions get old, the close quarters and lack of privacy irritating. People say and do things out of character. Relationships are strained. Men's ability to forgive, speak the truth in love, confront another person and love unconditionally will all be tested. Build relationships before you go.

6. *Cultural sensitivity.* One quick way to ruin a trip is for a team member to use a word of slang or a phrase that is inappropriate for the country, or to act in a way that is disrespectful of the host country. In the Philippines, for example,

you don't wave to a person and indicate for them to come to you as you would in America. To wave in this fashion is how you call a prostitute in the Philippines. Read as much as you can and talk to veteran missionaries in order to develop sensitivity to the customs and culture of the country you serve.

7. *Debriefing*. It is easy when the trip is over to check it off as another project completed, and to move on to the next thing. But your men's world has been shaken. They will need some time to readjust, come down to earth. Make the project a real growth experience by allowing plenty of debriefing time before coming home. Have each one share the highlight of his trip and how he was challenged in his Christian walk. Ask them to explain what steps they will take to become world Christians. Have them think about their response to questions Christian and non-Christian friends and family back home will ask, such as, "How was your trip?" and have them prepare a thirty-second answer. Take time to evaluate every aspect of the trip to discover what can be done better or differently next time. Debriefing not only brings closure to the trip but marks a new beginning for your men as they return home changed persons.

8. *Family involvement*. A man should only agree to go on a trip if his wife is in favor of it. As the planning process moves forward make sure the men keep their wives informed. A phone chain for the wives while the men are gone can be helpful, as is distributing faxes or messages that come in from the team. A church in Chicago assigned men from the church to shovel the driveway of each team member's home when necessary. What a great way to support the families!

9. *Churchwide support*. Some guys won't want to send out support letters asking for money. Some don't need to. But they should realize the letters aren't just about money. They are meant to share the vision of missions with others. If a man doesn't need to raise funds, have him send out a prayer letter instead of a support letter. Use your trip to fire up people beyond the team itself.

10. *Flexibility*. I know, I said it before. But I needed a tenth point to make it an official top-ten list. And not only that—it needs to be repeated.

Short-term missions is a ministry that takes a lot of time to plan and carry out. But the impact it can have on your men's ministry is measureless. Let me close this section with the warning I put on all of our mission brochures.

Warning:
Involvement in Men's Short-Term Missions
will cause world vision to spread
throughout your life and your ministry.

Evangelism Teams

Surveys of evangelical Christians show that only about twenty-five percent have been trained in evangelism and only about five percent have shared their faith with another person. I don't know about you, but I sure wouldn't want to go to battle with only a quarter of the soldiers having been trained and only one in twenty with any experience. Yet that is exactly what is happening in our churches today. Evangelism is an often overlooked area of men's ministry. In Chapter 6, I spoke about including evangelism as one of the components of a balanced ministry. In this section I want to mention a few things you can do to enhance this area of your ministry. Like a vacation with a purpose, once you get men sharing their faith with other men, their excitement grows as they spend time on the front lines. They get caught up in what God is doing in the lives of other men and in their own lives as well. You *can* form evangelistic teams—but the real goal is to develop an environment that makes evangelism an everyday part of being a Christian—and a normal part of the men's ministry. Here are some things you can do to make it happen:

1. *Cultivate an evangelistic mindset*. From the first day you

begin your ministry, remind the men of why you exist. This is much bigger than making men better husbands or fathers or more efficient workers. It's about doing kingdom business. It's about seeing men come into a relationship with Jesus and grow in it.

Make sure your men realize you aren't just going to make meetings and a program for them to come to and feel better about life. You do things so they can bring someone else in on their elbow, so they can be equipped to tell others about what Jesus has done in their life. A meeting doesn't go by that I don't remind the guys of why we gather. If they just want a nice little boys' club they can count me out. I realize that in some churches you face a circle-the-wagons mentality. It may take some time to break through that, but if you start from the beginning it's a little easier.

2. *Train your men.* Be creative. You don't have to announce a mandatory thirty-week course on evangelism. You can do a few things to make it more palatable. You could, for example, tell each of your small group leaders that sometime in the next two years you want their groups to study a book on evangelism. Books such as *How a Man Stands Up for Christ*[6] by Jim Gilbert, *How to Give Away Your Faith* by Paul Little,[7] *Becoming a Contagious Christian* by Bill Hybels and Mark Mittelberg,[8] *Lifestyle Evangelism* by Joseph Aldrich,[9] and *I Believe in Evangelism* by David Watson[10] are all great for small group use. The Navigators video series *Living Proof*[11] is also a great series for groups. By doing evangelism training through a small group or Top Gun group you aren't asking for another commitment from the guys. You're fitting the training into something they're already doing.

Make your training practical. Have your men write out their testimony and then give it to a couple of others in the group and allow them to critique it. I would do the same with a Gospel presentation. It isn't enough just to read the material and know it. You want them to practice explaining what they believe in a safe environment. Within that safe environment they can make mistakes, try different styles and get constructive, loving feedback.

Emphasize that evangelism flows out of relationships. This goes back to what we said at the start. A good men's ministry begins with men developing relationships with other men. Out of these relationships naturally flow evangelistic opportunities. Most men think they have to become someone they aren't when they share their faith. If we can help men see that God will use exactly who they are and what they have been through to reach other men with similar backgrounds, we have accomplished a great deal. A second emphasis for your training is that evangelism is a process. So often we're so interested in closing the deal that we forget Jesus described coming into a relationship with Him as a process of sowing, watering and harvesting. A final emphasis for a class like this is that the men must leave their comfort zone if they expect to be effective. You can't catch fish from your porch. You have to get in your boat and go to where the fish are. The fish don't come to you.

3. *Form a "special forces" team.* In time you will begin to notice the men who really do have the gift of evangelism. They love to meet with other men to tell them about Jesus. You may want to start a separate ministry for that group of men. We call our group "Ambassadors." It is their job to contact any new male member of the church and to welcome him to the ministry. They have also been equipped to meet with other men one-on-one to take their spiritual temperature and to encourage them to move forward from wherever they are in their experience with Jesus. Interestingly enough, most of the guys on this team are salesmen. They love to be with people. They aren't afraid of rejection. I would love to see an entire army of men on the streets of Milwaukee meeting with other men just to encourage them and speak boldly to them. The team you put together could adopt much different strategies and methods than our group, but it should still aim at telling others about Jesus.

4. *Use your special events as evangelistic opportunities.* Without getting into too much detail, you can pick one or two special events in the course of your year to deliberately seek to reach the unreached. In Appendix B, I describe fifteen great special events, some of which are evangelistic. Any well-planned breakfast, lunch or barbecue, however, can be a great way to gather men together and bring them an inspirational message focusing on the Gospel. Having too many of these causes them to lose their effect. But providing one or two a year can bring great results.

The heart of the issue in both mission trips and evangelism is whether or not your men's ministry is being proactive. To bring the fire home to your church means building men who are so on fire for Jesus that others are attracted to the fire—and those with the fire seek to share what they have.

Exercise 1—Special Teams Ministry

1. Share with the other leaders any cross-cultural experiences you have had and how they have impacted you as a Christian.

2. Considering the men in your church, what type of trip would be most appropriate?

3. What potential sources do you have for gathering information for future mission trips?

4. When in your yearly schedule would be a good time to have a trip?

5. What must you do to get started planning a trip?

6. What is your level of commitment to evangelism in your ministry? How is this evidenced?

7. How can you most effectively train men in evangelism within your existing program?

Notes

1. Chris Eaton and Kim Hurst (Colorado Springs: NavPress, 1991).
2. Monrovia, Calif.: Short-Term Missions Advocates, 1987.
3. David Bryant (Ventura, Calif.: Regal Books, 1979).
4. Bob Sjogren (Seattle, Wash.: YWAM Publishing, 1992).
5. Bill and Amy Stearns (Minneapolis, Minn.: Bethany House Publishers, 1995).
6. Jim Gilbert (Minneapolis, Minn.: Bethany House Publishers, 1996).
7. Paul Little (Downers Grove, Ill.: InterVarsity Press, 1988).

8. Bill Hybels and Mark Mittelberg (Grand Rapids, Mich.: Zondervan, 1994).
9. Joseph Aldrich (Portland, Ore.: Multnomah Press, 1986).
10. David Watson (Grand Rapids, Mich.: Eerdman's Publishing, 1976).
11. Based on the book by Jim Peterson (Colorado Springs, Colo.: NavPress, 1990).

Conclusion

In the opening chapter of this book I talked about the fields that are ripe for harvest—about the fact that everywhere we look we see men who are friendless, emotionally isolated, success-driven and spiritually hungry. These are men ready to respond to the Gospel and ripe to get involved in a men's ministry based in the local church.

This truth was brought home to me powerfully on Saturday morning, February 3, 1996. As a bit of background, let me tell you that over the past year we have seen steady growth in our monthly Saturday morning meetings. We started with 110 men attending in the fall, and by January had 155. Needless to say, the guys running the breakfast were excited. In our committee meeting last month we boldly projected we should plan for 175 men in February. That's a lot of eggs—but not much trouble having those on hand. Where to put that number of men was another issue.

The week before the February meeting the temperature in Milwaukee never got above 0°F. Wind chills ranged from −50° to −75°. Schools closed because of the danger the cold would pose to kids walking to school or waiting for a school bus.

I woke up at 5:30 A.M. on Saturday and listened to the cancellations on the radio, expecting my daughter's park-and-rec basketball game to be called off. While listening to an endless list of non-events, I leaned over to Colleen and asked if she thought they would cancel our men's breakfast. "Hey," she said out of her sleep, "if it was to be canceled, *you* would have had to call it in." So I got up and went to church.

Saturday was officially the coldest day of the year: −28° with a −75° wind chill. The cooking committee was fixing food when I walked into the kitchen at 7:00. Because of the cold they had decided only to cook enough for a hundred men. With the meeting scheduled to start at 7:30, there were only half a dozen men there at 7:15. I mumbled to myself that I would be leading a small group discussion instead of speaking to the usual large audience. I went up to my office to pray and go over my notes. When I came down at 7:45, more than 220 men were crammed into the fellowship hall—eating, sharing, laughing and enjoying one another's company.

We had a great time of worship that morning. I spoke about the stumbling blocks men face today and then gave time for discussion and prayer at the tables. It was an incredible morning. When I looked out over this great gathering of men of all ages and backgrounds, I was reminded once again: *The fields are ripe for harvest.* Men are hungry. They are looking for truth. For relationships with other men. For a life-changing experience. They are looking to have even the tiniest flicker of faith fanned into a raging fire. There is no doubt that the hottest place in Milwaukee that cold, cold February day was the fellowship hall of Elmbrook Church, where a fire lit many years ago was still burning bright.

As I survey the landscape of our society—its trends, values, and outlook—I am more convinced than ever that the time is right for every church in this country to have a ministry to men. It isn't enough for men to go to a weekend retreat or a Promise Keepers Conference or a missions trip—all good things in their own right. What men need now, more than ever, is a place where they can plug in with other men—week in and week out. Where they can be encouraged, comforted, challenged, held accountable and taught together. A place where they can be sharpened—in their marriages, their integrity, their prayer life, their use of God-given gifts. Where the fire can be lit or re-lit. The fire of their faith in Jesus, the fire of their marriage, the fire of their friendships. Men, it is time to bring the fire home to the church.

Appendix A:
Top Gun Ministry

In the winter of 1991–92, I was asked by our senior pastor to lead the Men's Ministry at Elmbrook Church. After surveying many men and talking to a number of leaders ministering to men around the country, I assembled some somber findings. It was obvious that the church in America was shallow, superficial and spectator-based—especially with respect to the men. I saw the need to develop leadership among our own men, and I set out to write a curriculum that would help men to go deep—deep in their relationship to the Lord, deep in their relationship to their spouse, and deep in their relationships to other men. I wanted to build a program that was an inch wide and a mile deep.

I fully realized I had to get away from the numbers game that is so easy to play. As Robert Coleman says in his wonderful book *The Master Plan of Evangelism*, Jesus didn't work to reach the masses by himself. He worked to build men to reach the masses. When the fields are ready for harvest, men need to be equipped with a vision and know-how to reap the harvest. The result was the development of a program called *Top Gun*. It has the following characteristics:

1. A *small group format*. Top Gun forms groups of 10–12 men who meet weekly for two hours, for a period of thiry-two weeks.

2. A *Relational Component*. During the first hour of a Top Gun small group meeting, the men divide up into groups of three or four for sharing, prayer and accountability. It is during this time that the

walls come down and men can be vulnerable with one another.

3. A *righteousness training component.* We aren't just interested in men acquiring more skills, but rather attaining to godliness.

4. A *service emphasis.* Not only is the group required to do two service projects over the course of the year, but each man makes a commitment to be active serving within the local church by the time the course is completed. During the third module of the curriculum, Servant Leadership, men do spiritual gift assessments that help them discover where they should plug into service in their church.

5. A *leadership component.* The nine-month equipping process is designed to encourage and equip men to provide leadership, based on sound biblical principles, in each area of their life—home, work, community, church and the world.

We started Top Gun in the fall of 1992 with two groups. I took one of the groups and one of my deacons took another group. I wrote as we went, and at the end of the year I was really unsure what type of effect it had on the men who participated. When we did our evaluations with all of the participants, I asked if any of them would be interested in leading a group next year. Sixteen men said they would. That was all the answer we needed. Knowing we wouldn't get enough men for sixteen groups, we had the men co-lead, which we felt was something the Lord orchestrated. Since that time we have seen incredible growth both at our church and in thirty churches across the country. In the fall of 1995 more than 150 men signed up to go through what is a rigorous course. For the rest of this section, allow me to share some of the basic aspects of our Top Gun Ministry (TG).

Purpose of Top Gun

1. *To share Life* (1 Thessalonians 2:8–9). The small group format allows men the chance to be encouraged, challenged, comforted, prayed for and held accountable. It becomes more than just a sharing of information. It is sharing life with one another. It is a chance for men to develop solid friendships with other men. It is a chance for them to share wounds, dreams, failures and successes that they perhaps have never shared with anyone else. One of the desired outcomes of the course is that men would see the need to participate in a small group setting the rest of their lives.

2. *To grow in Christ* (Colossians 2:5–7). It is possible to spend time with other men and never get around to really seeking after godliness. The stated purpose of TG is to help men grow closer to Jesus,

to increase their love for Him, and to reflect Him to the world in which they live. There is a heavy emphasis on the spiritual disciplines and on living a consistent lifestyle. One of the desired outcomes of the course is that men would have a daily devotional time with the Lord.

3. *To be equipped to influence others* (Ephesians 4:11–12). The course is designed to help men discover, develop and deploy their spiritual gifts. Every man who calls himself a Christian has a spiritual gift. We want to help him find out what it is and then use it to its fullest. As already mentioned, one of the desired outcomes is that men who have finished the course would serve somewhere in the local church.

How Top Gun Benefits Churches

1. *It develops leadership.* When I started the men's ministry I had about eight leaders. Four years later, I have more than eighty men working in the men's ministry, and many more have gone on to serve in other ministries of our church. When I am consulting with other churches and doing all-day seminars on how to start and run an effective men's ministry, one of the things I suggest is that they use TG to develop their leadership. There is nothing wrong with taking a year to develop a nucleus of guys who will be the future leaders of your ministry. The same holds true for a church. TG is a great tool for a pastor to use to develop the leadership within his congregation.

2. *It moves men out of the pews and onto the field.* For many years the only place you would see men serving was ushering or mowing the church lawn. The TG course helps men appreciate the true nature of servanthood and then to realize that they have a gift they can use in a local congregation.

3. *It starts men growing in Christ.* One of the complaints I hear on a regular basis is that men are tired of just getting together with other men over breakfast and sharing what is new in the world of sports. They say that before they got involved in TG they wanted to grow in Christ but didn't know how. Unfortunately, most men think they are more mature than they really are. The other group has the Peter Pan syndrome—they just don't want to grow up. As a result, men need something to help them cover the basics of Christianity and get grounded in the disciplines of prayer, Bible study, Scripture memorization, solitude, service and fellowship.

4. *It provides the next step for men after a Promise Keepers Conference.* One of the comments I hear in my travels is, "Promise Keep-

ers was great, but when I got home there was nothing." TG has been described as "Promise Keepers every week of the year." It is easy for a man to come home from a mountaintop experience like PK and settle in to his old lifestyle. A program like TG is easily transferable to your church setting and brings the fire home that was lit at the conference.

5. *It starts new small groups.* When a group gets done with the nine-month curriculum we challenge them to stay together and continue on as a small group. We have launched many small groups this way. Because for nine months the men have been together, had a retreat together, and served together, it is only natural that they become a small group. They can meet for an hour or so a week and go through one of the many study books available to men today. So in a way, TG is an effective launching pad for your small group ministry.

How We Accomplish Our Goals

There are a number of resources we bring together to help the men realize the goals of the Top Gun program.

Top Gun Manual. Each man receives a three-ring binder containing six modules. The modules have anywhere from four to seven lessons in them. The modules they study are:

>Intimacy With Christ
>Evangelism
>How to Study the Bible
>Building Your Family on Biblical Principles
>Servant Leadership
>Building Your Work on Biblical Principles

Every lesson has the stated goals for that lesson, an assignment, a Bible study, discussion questions for the small group sharing time, and discussion questions for a large group discussion.

Audiotapes. Each man receives a tape binder with nine cassettes that are used over the course of the year. The tapes, which include presentations by a number of Christian leaders from around the country, supplement the program's reading.

Books. Each module is coupled to a particular reading book that the men read and discuss over the course of the specific module. During the first module, "Intimacy with Christ," the men read Bill Hybels' book *Too Busy Not to Pray.*

How Your Men's Ministry Can Start Top Gun

In an ideal world, I would love for anyone who is going to lead a TG group to go through a TG group first, but I realize this is impossible. If you live in the Midwest you may wish, however, to attend a TG Leadership Training Seminar, which we offer twice a year. In just four hours you receive all the training you need to start groups in your church. By the fall of 1996, we will also have available training videos that you can use with the Leadership Manual to train a small group of potential leaders. When we train our own leaders, we meet on three consecutive Monday evenings for a couple of hours, an adequate amount of time to cover the material. If you have questions about the TG ministry and how you can use it, call or write to:

Steve Sonderman
Elmbrook Church
777 S. Barker Rd.
Brookfield, WI 53045
(414) 786–7051

In summary, of everything we have done in our men's ministry, Top Gun has had the greatest impact in the lives of our men. It generates an excitement that is contagious and its life-changing power brings glory to God. The greatest testimony to TG comes from the wives of the men who are in it. A week doesn't go by when I don't receive a letter or phone call from a wife telling me what a change TG is making in their marriage and life. For me, that is all the encouragement I need.

Appendix B: 15 Great Special Events

In this appendix I would like to provide you and your leadership team with several ideas for special events for your ministry. All the events here have been tested with our men or those of another church. (Don't worry—I'm not just making these up for the fun of it!) For each event I give a basic description, a reason to do it, and some guidelines to ensure its success.

One note: We have learned that men often won't come the first time you do something. They want to hear how it went and find out whether it's worth bringing a friend to. It's important, then, to do what you do with excellence so you can build confidence among your men that you will provide a quality event.

The events are not in any specific order.

1. Golf Outing

What: The men of your church and their friends spend an afternoon playing golf at a local course. You may want to consider having a lunch beforehand or a dinner after golf. We have had a speaker each time, as well as testimonies from the men on how God has used the men's ministry in their own growth. If you have the speaker at lunch, it gives the men a chance to talk with their guests about what was said while they are playing. We have also included wives for dinner afterward and found both men and their wives appreciated the event.

Why: A golf outing can be just for the men of your church—for a time of fellowship—or it can be an outreach event. You can encourage men to bring friends from work or the neighborhood to expose them to other Christians and a Christian message.

Guidelines:

1. Plan far in advance with the golf course. Not many can handle a lunch or dinner.
2. Settle on a purpose and make sure your men know why you are doing the event.
3. If you do a lunch, make sure the food providers know you are on a tight schedule.
4. Have the rules for whatever game you are playing on the carts ahead of time (if you play "best ball," for example, have the rules typed up and run off ahead of time).

2. Father/Child Canoe Trip

What: Your trip can be as short as a day and as long as a week, depending on what you want to do. It can be a simple float on a local river to a white-water trip. We have tried a variety of formats and it seems to work best as a long weekend—leaving early Friday, putting in that afternoon and then pulling out Sunday morning and traveling back on Sunday afternoon.

Why: Combining camping and canoeing is an excellent way for a dad and child to foster their relationship. It is a chance for them to hang out in a more rustic setting away from distractions and to really talk and work together.

Guidelines:

1. Use an outfitter that provides camping and canoeing equipment. Many Christian camps can provide a reasonably priced trip for you. If you go to one of the more popular canoeing areas in the country, there are also local outfitters who can help you.
2. Have a what-to-bring list available for the dads. A good outfitter provides these.
3. Have everyone put their sleeping bags and clothes in plastic bags. (I speak from experience on this one!) A duffel by itself will not—let me repeat, *will not*—keep your gear dry if it goes in the water. Do I need to repeat that again?
4. Be realistic about what you and your group can cover each day. We have learned that kids under ten can only handle three or four hours on the water a day. Extra time at the camp is a great way for bonding to take place.

5. Build into each day a devotional time for the dads and children to break away and talk about certain things. For example: In one session, have them share what they appreciate most about each other. It is helpful to guide the discussions.

3. Father/Child Bike Trip

What: Like the canoe trip, there are many ways to do this—from a one-day excursion beginning and ending at church to a week-long trip for hardcore cyclists. It can include camping or more comfortable arrangements such as a church camp or a hotel.

Why: This is a great relationship builder between a father and one of his children.

Guidelines:

1. This is probably an event for children who are at least junior high age. Our own junior high ministry runs a fairly demanding trip kids can do during the summer after their seventh grade year.
2. Again, use an outfitter that can provide you with safe, dependable equipment. Check with local bike shops and Christian camps.
3. You will have a better time if you can shuttle equipment in a couple of vans—"sag wagons"—rather than carrying all of it on your bikes.
4. Encourage the participants to work out before the trip so the first day doesn't kill them.
5. Have plenty of spare tubes. May I repeat—loads of extra tubes.

4. Men's Retreat

What: A retreat is an ideal opportunity for the men of your church or just a small group of men to get away for a night or two of fellowship, instruction and play. You can do many different types of retreats—a teaching retreat, a play retreat or a personal growth retreat. Decide up front what you want to do. I speak at retreats at least once a month and have found them incredibly helpful to men's ministries everywhere.

Why: Retreats provide a man a chance to get away from the distractions and pressures of life—to relax and be refreshed. They can also provide an opportunity for concentrated teaching on a specific area relevant to men.

Guidelines:
1. Decide on your purpose and clearly carry it through in your planning and publicity.
2. Use a facility where the accommodations are appropriate for men of all ages. I have been to rustic retreats where it was difficult to sleep. Needless to say, that doesn't go over well with most men. A nicer camp or even a hotel is a better place for a retreat—unless you deliberately choose a "rough it" weekend and advertise as such.
3. Plan your retreat a year in advance. You need ample time to schedule a location and line up a speaker.
4. Potential Schedule

   Friday Evening
   5:00   Registration
   7:00   Large Group (introduction to weekend, worship, teaching, testimonies, crowd breaker)
   8:15   Small Groups (a chance to get to know one another and to talk about what the speaker discussed)
   9:00   Free Time

   Saturday
   7:00   Devotions (supply one for those who aren't sure what to do)
   8:00   Breakfast
   9:00   Large Group (worship, testimony, speaker)
   10:15   Small Groups
   11:00   Free Time
   12:00   Lunch
   1:00   Free Time
   5:30   Dinner
   7:00   Final Session (worship, testimony, speaker)
   8:30   Go Home

5. Leave plenty of time for the guys to unwind and spend time with the Lord and with one another. There is nothing worse than going on a retreat and coming home more tired than when you left.

5. Barbecue

What: This event is an evening of food, fellowship, and fun. You might want to use it as a kickoff for your fall program. It could include a pig or chicken roast, music and a short program. Do it at church, a park, in a big backyard.

Why: Barbecues are low-key events that give men on the fringe an opportunity to see what your ministry is doing as well as to spend some time with other men from the church.

Guidelines:

1. If you use this as your ministry kickoff, be careful in your planning that you don't interfere with anything else on the church calendar.
2. Build into your schedule a chance for testimonies and an explanation of what the ministry is all about. You may want to pass out a calendar for the year, or show slides of last year's activities.
3. If you do something elaborate like a pig roast, consider hiring a caterer.

6. Kickoff Event

What: This event can look entirely different from church to church, but its purpose is to get your men's program off to a flying start in the fall. It could be a concert, an evening program with a keynote speaker, a cookout, etc. Be sure to include testimonies from men who have benefited from whatever ministry you have done up to that point, and have your leadership team share the vision of the ministry and what is happening in the coming year. This can also be a main event to sign up men for a small group.

Why: To kick-off the men's program. To introduce the men of your church to what is going on in the coming year and how they can be involved.

Guidelines:

1. Plan your kickoff far enough away from the start of school so you aren't competing with school and church events.
2. Have a flyer/brochure available that outlines upcoming activities for your ministry.
3. Have it be a low-key activity with plenty of time for guys just to hang out and talk with one another.

7. Outreach Breakfast or Lunch

What: This is an event designed specifically for evangelism. A great format is an event between an hour and an hour and a half in length. It includes a meal, a testimony by someone in the community—an athlete, businessperson, entertainer, etc.—and a clear Gospel presentation. Your goal is to develop a safe environment for this to take place. Each year we do a "Breakfast of Champions" at a local hotel on a Saturday morning. The men of our church pool together to buy tickets for a table—spots for six to eight guys—and bring their friends.

Why: An outreach meal is a chance for men to bring unchurched people to hear a clear presentation of the Gospel. Often men have shared their own testimony with a friend, but they need another person to share it as well.

Guidelines:

1. Potential Schedule
   8:00–8:10   Arrive and find your table
   8:10–8:15   Emcee welcomes men and prays
   8:15–8:45   Breakfast is served
   8:45–8:50   Special music
   8:50–8:55   Introduction of speaker
   8:55–9:25   Message/testimony
   9:25–9:30   Closing remarks
2. Encourage your men to come only if they are bringing another man.
3. Have the small groups in your ministry buy up tables.
4. Do a study on evanglism before this event, giving your men an opportunity to use what they have learned.
5. Don't have singing or anything else that needlessly makes visitors feel uncomfortable.
6. Choose a restaurant you know will do a first-class job. Make sure the waitresses are instructed not to pick up plates during the message.
7. Make up an invitation men can use to invite other men.

8. Sporting Event

What: With this event you gather a group of men and go to a sporting event together—a basketball, football, baseball, hockey or soccer game. By going out to dinner or having a tailgate party, you add time to talk and develop relationships with the other men in the church.

Why: Sporting events are easy events for building relationships with other men.

Guidelines:

1. Check on group ticket rates. Some stadiums have alcohol-free

family sections that can make the evening more enjoyable.

2. Some clubs allow you to reserve a place in the parking area for a tailgate party.

3. Decide ahead of time if the men can bring their families, or if you want a men-only event. Both are great options, but head off the confusion that *will* arise if you don't decide beforehand.

9. Fishing Outing

What: This one-day to one-week event is another great way for the men of your church to build relationships. It is also a chance to give men normally not involved a taste of the ministry. Some groups have planned one-day fishing excursions and others have opted for longer trips. We have a group of men that heads north every spring for a long weekend of bass fishing. They have had the time of their lives. If you plan on going for more than a day or two, you may want to consider using an outfitter or going through a Christian camp that does fishing trips on a regular basis.

Why: To have fun together, to enjoy a hobby together, and to build relationships with other men.

Guidelines:

1. Provide a what-to-bring list if you go overnight or longer.

2. Make reservations far enough in advance if you choose to go to wilderness areas where you need permits. (In the Boundary Waters Canoe Area of Minnesota, for example, you need permits ahead of time.)

3. Provide assistance to the novices on what type of fishing gear they need and what you will be fishing for.

4. Have someone responsible for sharing devotions on a daily basis.

5. If you use your own camping and cooking equipment, make sure you check it thoroughly before you leave home.

10. Financial Weekend

What: A two-day seminar on money management for men or couples. You can prepare your own material, bring in a speaker, or use videotapes from nationally known experts. Ron Blue's weekend presentation for our men and their wives was extremely helpful. He covered such topics as the biblical base of money, developing a family budget, and saving for retirement.

Why: A financial weekend serves a number of purposes. It provides solid instruction on Christian stewardship. It helps men and women deal with an area of their marriage that is usually a major source of disagreement. And it's another way to reach people who may not normally come to a men's event.

Guidelines:

1. Use materials that take a balanced, biblical approach.
2. Provide enough time for couples to talk with each other about their specific financial situation.
3. Have a workbook to take notes and a folder to hold any extra materials that are available.
4. Check out what audio-visual equipment will be needed and make sure everything is in working order.

11. Steve Farrar Conference

What: Steve Farrar is a great example of a nationally known men's writer (*Point Man, Finishing Strong,* etc.) who also speaks to churches and city-wide weekend conferences. His conference, entitled "Riding for the Brand," provides men with practical, biblical principles for becoming a godly man, father and husband. You will want to mobilize a number of churches from your area to have Steve or another major speaker come in.

Why: This event is great for bringing in new men as well as providing instruction for the men of your church and community.

Guidelines:

1. Most major speakers schedule at least a year in advance.
2. These types of events are an excellent way to start small groups. After Steve spoke to our men's ministry, we started eight groups that all went through *Point Man.* A number of the groups are still going three years later.
3. Start talking to men's ministry leaders from other churches about sponsoring a joint event.

12. Regional Men's Rally

What: This event is a chance for all the men's ministries from a city or region to come together to worship, fellowship, pray, and receive instruction from God's Word. For the past three years we have had gatherings of men in the Milwaukee area. We started with 1,800 men, then went to 4,500 men, and this year we expect about 6,000 men for a Saturday evening rally. The nice thing about a men's rally is that it can flow from the efforts of local churches and can break down racial and denominational walls. With the Promise Keepers Conferences during the summer, a citywide conference in the winter is a good alternative.

Why: A regional men's rally challenges men to grow in their relationship with Jesus and to be involved in bringing others to Christ as well. It can really boost the men's ministries in a city.

Guidelines:

1. Develop a committee that represents a number of churches. You will need men to cover the following areas: prayer, registration, publicity, facilities, volunteers (greeters, ushers, ticket sales, etc.), program, technical support (audio, video, lighting), financial and food.
2. Start working on your speakers and musicians at least a year ahead of time. The further ahead you can work out these arrangementsthe better.
3. Work closely with all the men's ministry leaders in the city to get the word out and to rally support for it.
4. Have a prayer rally a couple of months ahead of time in preparation for the event.
5. Have a good balance of music, teaching, prayer and testimonies in the program.

13. Promise Keepers Summer Conference

What: Each summer Promise Keepers offers conferences around the country that begin on a Friday evening and run through Saturday evening. The conference includes great speakers, music and testimonies.

Why: PK Conferences can act as one of your men's ministries' special events. It is important not to use Promise Keepers as your whole men's ministry, but rather *one* of the things your ministry can use as a resource for instruction and fellowship.

Guidelines:

1. Plan ahead. These conferences usually sell out quickly, so you will want to order tickets for your church as soon as they go on sale.
2. Try to car pool together and stay at the same hotel so you can have the extra time for fellowship.
3. Ask your pastor ahead of time if you would be able to share on a Sunday morning what happened at the conference.

4. Have a follow-up meeting a month or so later where the men can share what God is doing in their hearts and you can share some potential next steps for them. One might be how they can get into a small group.

14. Sweetheart Banquet

What: An evening that the men's ministry hosts at a local restaurant or hotel banquet hall for the couples of your church. The program could include a nice dinner—complete with dinner music, of course—followed by a short program that might include a message for couples. Some groups get special prices for the hotel so a couple can say the night.

Why: To help guys plan something for their wives so they aren't surprised when February 14 comes around. Seriously, this can be a very special time for couples to get away and have a nice dinner and evening together with other Christian couples.

Guidelines:
1. If you are going to do it, do it right. Have it at a place that has a pleasant atmosphere and good food.
2. Work with the hotel to ensure everyone is served promptly and that waitresses aren't picking up dishes during the program.
3. Have your guys put it on their schedule far in advance.

15. Super Bowl Party

What: A party where men can invite other men to join them to watch the Super Bowl. For a smaller group this can take place at someone's home; for a larger group it could happen in the fellowship hall or gym of your church. Many groups are holding events centered around major sports events, and some churches invite professional athletes to do an evangelistic talk at half time. Another way to go is to order the special half time video that Sports Spectrum puts out each year. The video includes testimonies from NFL players and a clear presentation of the Gospel.

Why: Fellowship and outreach.

Guidelines:
1. Borrow or rent a large screen TV. Make sure it works!
2. Divide up responsibilities for the food.
3. Order your half-time tape in advance so it arrives in time for your men to preview it and decide how it will fit into your event.

Appendix C:
Resources for Ministry

SMALL GROUPS

Training materials for leaders

The Big Book on Small Groups by Jeffrey Arnold (Downers Grove: InterVarsity Press, 1992).

Brothers! Calling Men into Vital Relationships by Geoff Gorsuch (Colorado Springs: NavPress, 1994).

Good Things Come in Small Groups by Ron Nicholas (Downers Grove: InterVarsity Press, 1985).

How Dynamic Is Your Small Group? by Dave Seemuth (Wheaton, Ill.: Scripture Press, 1991).

Materials to use in a small group

Christian Growth

Design for Discipleship series—six books on the basics of Christianity (Colorado Springs: NavPress).

LifeChange series—study guides on Bible books (Colorado Springs: NavPress).

The Body: Being Light in Darkness by Charles Colson (Dallas: Word, 1992).

Daily Disciplines for the Christian Man by Bob Beltz (Colorado Springs: NavPress, 1993).

The Disciplines of a Godly Man by Kent Hughes (Chicago: Crossway Books, 1991).

How a Man Prays for His Family by John Yates (Minneapolis: Bethany House Publishers, 1996).

Knowing God by J. I. Packer (Downers Grove: InterVarsity Press, 1993).

Rediscovering Holiness by J. I. Packer (Ann Arbor, Mich.: Vine Books, 1992).

Too Busy Not to Pray by Bill Hybels (Downers Grove: InterVarsity Press, 1988).

What God Does When Men Pray by William Carr Peel (Colorado Springs: NavPress, 1993).

Who You Are When No One's Looking by Bill Hybels (Downers Grove: InterVarsity Press, 1987).

Husband/Fathering Issues

How a Man Prepares His Daughters for Life by Michael Farris (Minneapolis: Bethany House Publishers, 1996).

How a Man Prepares His Sons for Life by Michael O'Donnell (Minneapolis: Bethany House Publishers, 1996).

If Only He Knew by Gary Smalley and Steve Scott (Grand Rapids, Mich.: Zondervan, 1982).

Point Man by Steve Farrar (Portland, Ore.: Multnomah Press, 1990).

The Seven Secrets of Effective Fathers by Ken Canfield (Wheaton, Ill.: Tyndale, 1992).

Strategies for a Successful Marriage by E. Glenn Wagner and Dietrich Gruen (Colorado Springs: NavPress, 1994).

Men's Issues

Finishing Strong by Steve Farrar (Portland, Ore.: Multnomah Press, 1996).

Healing the Masculine Soul by Gordon Dalbey (Dallas: Word, 1991).

How a Man Faces Adversity by Robert Hicks (Minneapolis: Bethany House Publishers, 1996).

Man in the Mirror: Solving the Twenty-Four Problems Men Face by Patrick Morley (Nashville: Thomas Nelson, 1992).

The Seven Seasons of a Man's Life by Patrick Morley (Nashville: Thomas Nelson, 1995).

Tender Warrior by Stu Weber (Portland, Ore.: Questar, 1993).

Promise Builders Study Series (Denver: Promise Keepers).

Work

How to Balance Competing Time Demands by Doug Sherman and William Hendricks (Colorado Springs: NavPress, 1989).

How a Man Handles Conflict at Work by Paul Tomlinson (Minneapolis: Bethany House Publishers, 1996).

Keeping Your Ethical Edge Sharp by Doug Sherman and William

Hendricks (Colorado Springs: NavPress, 1990).

Your Work Matters to God by Doug Sherman and William Hendricks (Colorado Springs: NavPress, 1987).

LEADERSHIP

Developing the Leader Within You by John Maxwell (Nashville: Thomas Nelson, 1993).

In the Name of Jesus by Henri Nouwen (New York: Crossroads, 1993).

Leadership Is an Art by Max Depree (New York: Doubleday, 1989).

The Master Plan of Evangelism by Robert Coleman (Old Tappan, N.J.: Fleming Revell, 1963).

Ordering Your Private World by Gordon MacDonald (Nashville: Thomas Nelson, 1985).

Spiritual Leadership by J. Oswald Sanders (Chicago: Moody Press, revised 1994).

Transforming Leadership by Leighton Ford (Downers Grove: InterVarsity Press, 1993).

MISSIONS

How to Be a World-Class Christian by Paul Borthwick (Wheaton, Ill.: Scripture Press, 1993).

In the Gap by David Bryant (Ventura, Calif.: Regal Books, 1989).

Run With the Vision by Bob Sjogren and Bill & Amy Stearns (Minneapolis: Bethany House Publishers, 1995).

Stepping Out: A Practical Guide to Prepare for a Short-Term Mission Trip (Seattle: YWAM, 1992).

Unveiled at Last by Bob Sjogren (Seattle: YWAM, 1992).

Vacations With a Purpose: A Planning Handbook for Your Short-Term Missions Team by Chris Eaton and Kim Hurst (Colorado Springs: NavPress, 1991).

EVANGELISM

Becoming a Contagious Christian by Bill Hybels and Mark Mittelberg (Grand Rapids: Zondervan, 1994).

How to Give Away Your Faith by Paul Little (Downers Grove: InterVarsity Press, 1988).

How a Man Stands Up for Christ (Minneapolis: Bethany House Publishers, 1996).

Out of the Saltshaker and Into the World by Becky Pippert (Downers Grove: InterVarsity Press, 1979).

MEN'S ORGANIZATIONS

Christian Businessmen's Committee, 1800 McCallie Avenue, Chattanooga, TN 37404

The Gathering, 106 E. Church St., Orlando, FL 32801

Promise Keepers, P.O. Box 18376, Boulder, CO 80308, (303) 964–7600

The Navigators Business and Professional Ministries, Roger Fleming, P.O. Box 6000, Colorado Springs, CO 80934

Career Impact Ministries, 8201 Cantrell Road, Suite 240, Little Rock, AK 72207, (800) 4–Impact

Steve Farrar Ministries, 5950 Berkshire Lane, Suite 1020 LB53, Dallas, TX 75225, (214) 361–5511

National Center for Fathering, P.O. Box 1918, Manhattan, KS 66502, (913) 776–4114

Acknowledgments

Thank you to the men of Elmbrook, who have allowed me to try out these principles on them over the last five years.

Thank you to the fourteen Deacons and Coordinators of the men's ministry, who really run the show. It has been a great ride thus far, and I can't wait to see where God takes us next. I love each of you deeply and count it a great privilege to work alongside you.

Thank you to Stuart Briscoe, my senior pastor, boss and most importantly, friend. Your preaching led me to the Lord twenty years ago. You called me to serve at Elmbrook some twelve years ago and have given me the encouragement and freedom to do ministry since that time. You have lived and taught the principles found in this book.

Thank you to Dave H., a friend and mentor. Your godly counsel and wisdom allows me to do what I am doing.

Thank you to Diane, my former secretary, who encouraged me along the way, protected my schedule and helped organize the ministry for me.

To Dave and Kathy, Phil and Mary, George and Laurie, and John and Kris—our Couples Prayer Group. Over the past year, your faithful and fervent prayers have carried me through this project.

To Dave, Darryl, Bruno, and Lynn—the Christian Men's Ministry Committee. Thank you for allowing me to run ideas by you and for being such cheerleaders during the process.

Thank you to the Top Gun ministry team. You inspire me with your dedication and passion for ministry. Your love of life and one another. You are a living illustration of what men's ministry is all about, You truly get it.

Thanks to my brother Phil and good friend John for your weekly calls to check in and see how things were going and ask if there was anything you could do to help.

A huge thanks to Kevin Johnson, my editor at Bethany House Publishers. Thank you for believing in me and giving me the opportunity to do this project. Your patience, guidance, and encourgement will always be remembered and appreciated.

To my wife, Colleen, and my four wonderful children, Kristin, Angela, Tim, and Jon. Thank you for putting up with me when I went to my study to work on "the book." Each of you has been so excited about this book and I am proud to be your husband and father.